Treasured Moments with God

Lucille Cislak

COMPANION
PRESS

An imprint of
Genesis Communications, Inc.

Treasured Moments With God
by Lucille Cislak

Companion Press
An Imprint of Genesis Communications, Inc.
P.O. Box 91011 • Mobile, AL 36691
(888) 670-7463
Email: GenesisCom@aol.com

ISBN 1-58169-014-2
For Worldwide Distribution
Printed in the U.S.A.

Table of Contents

DEDICATION

To little children, who have allowed me to understand the simplicity of God.

To Paul, whose faith never wavers, and to Julie, the encourager.

I

JOY IN GOD'S STRENGTH

True Love

Blessed Holy Spirit, tell me of joy.

And He says:

Joy is sensed when you feel My presence. A beautiful sweeping flows through you—it encompasses you and My Spirit becomes magnified. You may begin to weep and smile, flowing in the presence of the Holy Spirit. Breathe Me in deeply. Feel My peace. Feel the calm; bathe in it.

Hear Me whisper, "I love you." Thank you for lending yourself to your Creator, so that I may engulf you with sweetness and unity. Don't be afraid to smile when it feels so good!

Put away your childlike games and come grow with Me. The joy you now feel is the true love. See how warm and pleasant it is, caressing your every motion? Praise be to the Spirit of God. Smile. Let it flow now from the inside out, continually, without ceasing, through good and through bad, because the joy of the Lord is for all time!

⸺ ◆ ⸺

Reaching God

Why do you carry this burden? Do I not watch over My churches? Do My eyes not see everything? Why then do you worry? Pray and be encouraged. Lift up your heart and ask Me what you will, but do not carry that burden. You are not to become heavy; otherwise you might stumble and fall. Lift up the things of the world in the spirit, and do not take them into your body.

Tell the others to avoid burdensome situations, for they too will stumble if they do not. If you follow My command, you will see that the work of the Spirit is not heavy. Your strength is in *what?* Your strength is in My joy. My joy is that which makes you shine! What thing can you change by becoming heavy? Is there even one situation?

Don't you see how you are made, and how I, the Lord, have equipped you for battle? The weapons I have given you are sufficient, so you need not wear yourself out by beating your breast and crying out. Put your petitions before Me, and know that I am the Lord and can do all things. Jesus within you will take your burden, and He will give you peace in its place. Come now and be willing to let go of your way, for it is tiresome and weary. But when you come to Me in song and praise, your every request will be heard in the heavens. My way is easy. What is your way?

———— ◆ ◆ ————

Child of Mine

For your days will be filled with merriment. Your days will be My days, for I am in you. You are like a flower in My sight, with blooms that open to My light. The heavens look upon you with radiant joy and love.

Most obedient child of Mine, why do you worry so? Don't you know I am at rest within you? Don't you know that you must not fear? Don't you know that I love you and tenderly care for you?

Spend no more of your precious time dwelling on things that do not concern Me, but dwell only on the things that are *of Me*.

O My beautiful child, you offer so much. Your heart is like gold to Me. On that glorious day when I come to you, I will have shining jewels prepared for you. You will smile and have a heart as light as a feather, and your grief will disappear.

You know I come to you only in life, beauty, and in all good things. Never despair, My child, for My warmth will always comfort you. Your life will remain as it is—in Me. On that glorious day when I take you home, you will know that you, beloved, have always known the truth, and you will share in that vision with Me throughout all eternity.

Blessings upon the most precious of My Father.

Increase in Power

My heart is overflowing because of you, a little one so eager to please. I have been taking inventory of your deeds and your willingness to act when I prompt you. Do you like the increase? It is what I told you I would give you. Do you remember? Higher ground with more of My breath—more of the power to move in My anointing and more precision. Do you feel the change in the degree of accuracy? Obedience is wonderful, isn't it?

Do you want to go higher? I already know you do. You are going to run with Me, and many others will also run with Me. This battle holds intense joy for those who understand and who allow Me to train them. I am joining you together even as you write. I am blowing them into various positions, and I will allow you to recognize this as My plan.

In these times, do not be concerned about anything. Understand and rest in what I'm saying to you. Carry no weights in the natural or in the spirit. I will need you to be empty and ready to respond. I can see your agreement in what I am saying to you. The revelation word, given in prophetic word and song, comes now. *Now* it comes! Suddenly, like clashing cymbals, it comes!

Be still; I am opening doors that have been sealed in the past, for this is the time in which I will remove the binding from the doors. I am releasing the prisoners from their chains. Feel My heart, know My heart, and understand the times. My children are being released to you and all who will receive them. Do not turn them away: They are Mine . . . they are Mine. This work will bring the greatest reward because it is, on your part, an act of mercy. Each time you feel that you are unable to complete the work, I will breathe new strength into you. Have no fear, because this work has been preordained—ordained before it comes to you. Sing, dance and shout, for the victory is yours! I have given it to you. Reach out to the prisoners, for I love them just as I love you. Rise up, my warriors. Rise up, my army.

Sound the alarm. Wave the victory flag. Go now and set them free in My name. Halleluia!

The Task

(2 Corinthians 12:9)

Be strong and let your strength show. Don't be afraid; I will guide you always. Trust in Me, believe in Me, and glorify My name. I am with you. The Spirit is heavy on your heart—by your tears, you know it is I. Blessings will be yours for what you have sown. Mercy and love are abundant in you. You are about My work, and you will do My work. You will be happy and strong, and have great understanding. Blessings and blessings you will reap with joy!

Many people *know of Me,* but *do not have Me* in their hearts. You are to tell them what I hold for them when they ask Me. My grace is with you, and you know now what I mean and where it is written, "My grace is sufficient for you." By grace, everything good in you has been given by Me—and I know you will never have shame for Me.

Because you are obedient, much will be put upon you, but it will not be too heavy for you to carry. You will do all things with joy. Remember, at all times you are being blessed. Speak to Me as you have, and I will continue to tell you things you cannot know but through Me. You have My blessing.

Be Encouraged

To be in the presence of the Father is great, but to live with Him is even greater. For you will be as a dove—so pure and lovely, so gentle and true. I tell you that there is much happiness awaiting you if you can only endure. To truly be with Me is not easy, for there is much work to be done and so little time. But I tell you that for every stone you lift in this world, you will be given a jewel in My kingdom.

God Is Everywhere

And I looked up at the sky and asked, *"God where are You?"*

And He said:

Everywhere—above your heart, under your feet, at your right and at your left. I surround your very being like the Light of lights. I am beauty and love; and because I made you, you will be perfection unto Me in My world. You will have a body of glory. Do you know what that is?

I said, *"No, Lord; will you tell me?"*
And He said:

Blessed one of so many questions, I will ever so surely answer them all.

You will be beautiful, but not in the same way you are now. For you will be as light, but not as a light you can picture in the world as you know it, for no man can paint My glory.

There will be many here that you will know; your memory will not leave you. Now, do not waste time on what has already been promised. Go now and do what I have commanded you to do on this earth. Come to Me at all times with prayer and questions; but do what must be done for My children, so that they will have nourishment in My world. Constantly put My name forth, for they must know truth. Be happy in My name, and let your joy show.

2

DEEP STRUGGLES

Hearing

I am still so rigid in so many ways, and not at all flexible to do what God wants of me. Oh, I think I am listening to Him, but He shows me that I must become still more pliable. I do not trust Him enough to completely let go of my own self-image, but He is helping me right now. Even as I write, the Spirit of the Lord is present, and He does move my pen. Glory to the Lord, where would I be if You had not saved me?

And He says:

Where are you now, and what must you do to obtain the riches of heaven? Are you not My Father's child? Are you not worthy to be called His own? You cannot gain anything by your own merits—no, not one thing. I do not ask you for good works; I ask only for obedience. But to be obedient, you must be able to hear. Where have you put your priorities? To do or to listen? I

9

watch you always, and I see how you are: You have arrogance where I desire humbleness. But do not judge yourself too harshly, because you do not know My ways. Be still within and My peace will come upon you. Let Me touch your heart. Do not criticize what I have done with you, and do not complain about what you have or do not have. Do not grumble about *anything*. I can see you are beginning to understand.

Oh, precious one, take time to know the Holy Spirit. You cannot own a mansion if you haven't enough for a room. So it is with the Spirit: You cannot be given more faith if you cannot care for what you already have. More will be given to him who has much, but little to him who has little—very little will be given to that one. I want to give you abundantly if you will only accept *and act upon* what I have already given you.

The knots that remain within you must be loosened. These knots represent burdens that should not be a part of you at all. These things that bind you are hindering the flow of My Spirit. How can you grow when you are entangled? So if you truly want more of Me, as you pray, you will let go of your worries. If you have given them to Me, do not then try to take them back.

Rest and allow Me entrance to your heart. Let your spirit become one with My Spirit in love and harmony. These things are made perfect through Me.

Show me, Lord, with Your eyes, every burden that I am to drop at your feet.

I Feel Your Pain

Hush little child—don't cry.
I'm right here by your side.
I know you feel alone.
And I know you are like an island:
Bewildered, bewildered, not understanding at all.
Your pain—I feel your pain;
Aggravation—I see it over you.
Come away, come away,
do not dismay any longer,
For I am with you. I hold you close.
I feel your pain. I see your face.
There's nothing about you I do not know,
And that is why you can count on Me.
I am the One to turn to
when you have no one else,
When others fall short of your needs.
See My wonderful plan for you:
I have made you to depend on me.
Don't be sad; don't be weary.
Don't fret—the moment is passing.
I'm so close to you that you can touch Me.

Yes, you can. . . . Yes—you can!
Don't think for a moment that I've left you:
My presence is within you.
I delight in your smile.
I wait to behold you.
I come to embrace you.
Take the time . . . all you need to receive Me,
For I am not hurried or restless.
I am patient. I am very patient.
Is that a smile I see
by the corners of your mouth?
Do your eyes now tear from relief?
It's over—it's all over.
Rest assured that I carried your storm away.
Just remember that I'm the One
who loves you—
No matter how far away you go,
And no matter how deep you have dug.
It's over. It's finished. It's done.

Anger

(2 Corinthians 12:9; *Ecclesiastes 1:9*)

In my weakness, I am made strong.

No, Sir, I am not—that's not true. I hate what has happened. I feel terrible, and I want to hide and disappear! I feel awful, like a mess. I want to cry, but I'm tired of that, too! So, now what do I do? Wait, I suppose, in my anger. Wait for what? An angel to come and say it's all right? What for? So what? Who cares? Not me—I'm sick of it, sick of striving—for what? So I can do some great thing? For what? For Jesus—why? I know about You now, but why? Nothing is the same, or is nothing different? Yes, everything is the same under the sun. Nothing has changed. I'm still here as I am, and trying things are still happening to me. All I seem to do is complain anyway! Why am I so transparent that I pour my heart out on paper? Probably for pride—what else? I hope whoever reads this book knows how weak I am, because that's the truth. To have some stupid, fake purpose in life— that's all. Is my life a joke? It's not funny—it hurts. I'm hurt. . . . I'm really hurt.

Who will understand, who will hold me? Please help me, for I can't help myself. I already know what's coming . . . It's about my strength—no, not my strength—but that I will be made strong. Listen for it; it's coming. . . . I feel it now, like a little calm, tiny breeze; a whisper, a little nudge. All right, so You're here. Now what are You going to do with me? I'm still a mess.

And the Spirit of the Lord says:

Be still, My child. Be still even as I hold you. Do not move about in your mind. Be still so I may have fellowship with you. Do you think I do not see your tears? Do you think I do not care? I see that you feel that way. Why do you take so much upon yourself? That is not My way. Look at how you are. Who has done this to you? Who do you blame? The enemy? You do not blame the enemy . . . do you? Did I cause this? You are the only one left. Are you so unhappy that you would throw away all that I gave you? If not, you must stop your behavior and change your mind. Your anger turns the angels away—do you know that? Your begrudging attitude closes doors.

In the midst of your storm, I was there, but you could not see Me. I see that you are listening now. You must rely on the peace I left with you when you received Me. That is the very thing you need. If you do not lean on the peace I gave you, you will fall, because your own understanding will not support you. My words are not many, but they are precise. You have the ability to accept My words as truth, or to accept your own. You must decide.

Are you a match for your Father? What more do you know? I do not say harsh words to rebuke you, but to bring you into a knowledge of the truth. You must stay focused on Me; otherwise I cannot use you! Do you understand? Do not get so caught up with the problems of this world, for they will always be; but set your mind and your heart on the things of the future. I speak of the future as your home with Me. Be aware of your old ways and deal with them as you should.

———•◆•———

Depression Expression

You have put your hope in the things of this world. I said to fix your vision on that which is to come, for there is no pain and heartache in the world you *will* live in. Be patient and calm. Quiet your tongue so that your spirit may speak. Don't be in such a rush; be still and your God will talk with you. Of course you cannot find fulfillment in this world, and you should not be surprised. Only in the death of the fleshly nature can you receive divine revelation. Are you slow to catch on? Perhaps, by the standard of the world, you are lacking; but by the standard of Jesus, you are *exceedingly filled* with every kind of gift.

You always take inventory of what you have and have not. How often do you look at what you *will have*, if only you will run the good race? I have created you for a purpose, and your destiny lies with Me. Stay in the boat and do not get out; otherwise the storm will sink you. If you will only stay in the boat, you will begin to see everything in a different way, and the fears you now have will all become still. Trust not in man, but only the One who saves.

———————◆◆◆———————

Sin and Reproof
(Philippians 4:13)

Surely I cannot do a wrong and ask forgiveness, since I knew it was wrong when I did it, knowing you knew I did it.

And He says:

Who have you wronged? Who have you hurt? Is there a lie? To whom have you lied? I tell you that you may come to Me in all circumstances. Do you think that what you have done is worse than murder? It is the same. Let us talk about it. Tell me where your heart is; tell Me what you feel. I see your pain, but I know the truth. Let nothing stand in your way as you come to Me. What is it you *think* you have done, and what have you actually done?

Father, why do you speak to me with so many questions? Can't you just tell me if I'm wrong; and if I am, will you tell me what to do? Help me, Jesus.

And He says:

How much will you lose to remain in My grace? How much of what you own would you let go of because of Me? *Some* of what you own? *Most* of what you own? *All* of what you own? I tell you that no man gives Me everything! But I ask no man for everything; I wish for all to prosper and not be without. But spiritually . . . spiritually I must have all of you. Do you understand?

Yes, but Lord . . . You're not telling me what to do. You have not even told me if I was wrong. I don't know if I'm supposed to repent or not.

He says:

Of what is there to repent? That you do not wish to be devoured by wolves? Did you ask for this? Were you, yourself, led to believe a lie? Heed My warnings about becoming involved with wolves—they seek to devour!

I want you to rest now. Lie down in the Spirit and rest; it has been enough for now. To answer your question, I tell you that no, you are not perfect before Me, nor will you ever be as long as you are in this world. But My love for you is no less now than when you will be made perfect. Don't be so concerned that you wish to hide your face from Me—the evil one waits for those moments! You are precious to me, child; I love you so much.

You asked for My help before this problem occurred. You asked Me to put words in your mouth; but when the time came, you spoke mostly on your own. So it is in the world: Your faith is not strong enough yet, but I am building you, and I will put My Spirit in you stronger than before. You will see and know the difference.

You have perseverance. You will also be given more wisdom, so that you might acquire more patience; you lack in this area, but I will build you up. Do your best not to go against My commands; but when you do, do not be afraid to come to Me. I am forever forgiving. My blessings are on your family. Remember that you can do all things through Christ.

Drifting Away

Stop looking to other people so that you might see approval in their eyes. But fix your eyes on Christ, who is your overseer. You have run into the muddy waters on the edge of the river. Why did you stray? Is My grace not sufficient for you? I see your frustration, anger and hopelessness, as if following My ways are for nothing. I watch you, and I know you have pity on yourself because of all your trials . . . and shake your head.

Well, rejoice! and again I say, rejoice! for the kingdom of the Lord is near. Can you really not persevere? Or do you tell yourself you cannot?

I know it is difficult to leave the mud—where you can feel your own feet—but now I ask you to come away from that. Trust in me, and let yourself drift back into the deep waters where *you* are no longer in control. Do not fear, for I will support you. Pull yourself loose and cling to Me. You see, your *own* desire to be discouraged has taken you from Me; you *chose* this.

Now you say, "Thank you God for this revelation," and you are quick to grab My hand. But have you forgotten something? You must repent for being disobedient, and ask for forgiveness; then all will go well with you.

Breaking Control

And I said to the Lord, *"I want to help someone, but how and when do I know the point at which to stop? How do I find the line between helping or being controlling? Where is the line? When do I stop?"*

And He says to me:

My child, you are forever asking questions, but this desire to know the truth is a good thing. I see your heart and how you long to do good. When you reach out to a brother or sister in love, you are doing My work, and My words will flow through you. You already know this truth.

When you receive tightness in your spirit at any time, My Spirit is not at work, but the force of the evil one is. He wishes to weaken you with feelings of inadequacy and hopelessness. When the assuredness of My Spirit leaves you and feelings of demand come into you, you are standing on the line of good and evil.

Other people will not crumble if you pull away to spend time with Me. No, they must learn to walk as you have. Have mercy on others. Have concern, not contempt. Have a desire, not a demand. Have bold humbleness, but not hostility. Finally, have love in correction, not control. These things are necessary, as I desire to spend more time with you in spirit, because if you are overly busy about a brother's business, then you have little time for Me.

Glory be to the Lamb who was slain for your ungodliness. Glory be within you, in spirit and in truth. Let everything that you do, have life! Remember that I am the Giver of life. Be steadfast in My Word, and do not sin.

Don't Pull Away

For your ways are not My ways. Look, I am here—even as you are. I see a cloud between you and Me; the cloud represents separation. Why do you separate yourself from Me? What have I done to you that you should turn away from Me, child that I love? You are *not* as low as you say you are. My angels have charge over you, and your ways are not My ways.

Look, I hold before you a gift, a wonderful gift. Do you want it? It is free, but it came with a price. The price was not for you to pay. It has already been paid for by the One who loves you.

I Will Help You

Come here, child. Put your hands in My hands. Don't you know that I love you? Because I see what you have need of, it is not necessary for you to bring it before My face. I say, Put it at My feet, because I see your situation before you are able to cry out because of it. Don't waste time in idle turmoil, but do as I have commanded: Love one another. If you will just do that, you will allow Me free rein to work on your behalf. When the situation becomes your focus, at that moment you have no need of Me.

Understand that I am by your side always in absolute love for you, but I cannot work in the midst of sin. If there is hatred in your heart, how can My will be done? You make the choice, not I. Remember: I have given *you* authority! What is your focus? What has your attention? Is it the problem you are now facing in your life? Or is it Me and My glory?

Understand the deep things in order to overcome the trivial. You see, dear one, My provision is always here for you, because it is My will to give it to you. I will not deny you anything that is in accord with My will. My will is simple.

How do men know that you are of Me? How do *you* know that you are of Me? See, it is simple: Learn to pay attention to stillness. Learn to listen quietly in your spirit. Are you able now, for this time, to put your problem at My feet? Love those who persecute you because of Me, because I also love them. Don't tell Me what is wrong; tell Me what you *want*. I will give to you *out* of your love for Me.

Why Do They Scoff at Me, Lord?

The blind can see where the sighted cannot. The deaf can hear where the hearing cannot. The lame shall seek, and they will find Me through those who speak My Word.

Don't be saddened by the stiff faces of men, for they think they have in their head what you have in your heart. When you come to Me, I take away your pain and give you understanding. By quietly living your faith, you will remain strong, while those who boast of their faith have none. Pity those who willingly choose not to know Me, for they will answer when they are called to Me. I seek not to destroy but to love, and I seek not one group but all. Those who will not share Me as they share their bread will not have Me in their hearts. It is sad what some men choose, for they will not know divine heaven.

Blessed are you who have Me and put Me before the thrones of men, for in the end, it is *you* who will wear the crown. I tell you this of those who think they are greater than you: Their knowledge is worthless when compared to the blessings you hold in your heart. And blessings will be yours because you hold the truth and will not be shaken.

———◆◆———

Grow With Instruction

I want you to do what is right concerning everything in my life. I am perplexed about whether or not I am in Your will. If I am to keep the law, then I cannot break the law, because You said to keep the laws of men. How can I say this of God when . . . ?

He says:
Would you listen if I talked with you? Would you hear the reproof of your Father? If you can, then I will tell you.

There was a man of no money. Now there was another man who was wealthy. Who do you suppose could help the other? If you said the man with the money, you are correct, for how can a beggar help a rich man?

But I say unto you this day that no one can help the rich man because he is blind. To those who have much, much more will be given. The man who is rich in Me will surely prosper, but the one who is rich in the world will die as a beggar with nothing. Are they both My children? Yes. Do I love them equally? Yes. Why, then, do you worry about the things of this world? There is nothing you can change, not even yourself. It is *all* up to Me. I am the Father, and I will care and provide for all of My children, from the least of them to the most. I will guide you and lead you, lest you go astray.

You say you are afraid of Me. Why, then, do you stand in front of Me with so many questions? Get behind Me and follow! You are not to suggest to Me what we shall do; but I will do it if you get out of the way. Why do you continue to stand there? I am your shield, and I will go before you and bless all that you do. Yes, then you will do it—but from behind Me; then, and only then, will you be in My perfect will. Is that what you want? Stay in your proper position lest you fall. Seek Me in all things; then I will bring to you those that are of Me and bring about those things that I want to bless. Do not move quickly on your own. Do not speak that which is not yours to speak. I will put My words into each one as I see fit.

Remember, I need you to be a vessel, not a vassal. You will learn the difference between these two words.

My grace abounds in you, My light shows forth through your eyes, and My mercy is upon you. You will grow and have understanding.

My Concern?

Lord, he won't listen to me.

And He says:

For he does not know the source of what you say—Me—and he does not care to. For all your concern, he has none, for your heart is of Me and My will. He has no concern for that, but only of himself.

Don't you know that one cannot hear or believe what one does not already know? Let him be and do not worry, for he will be dealt with by Me in My time.

Worry not for those who do not know Me, but remember to keep yourself strong, for your strength will be necessary in times to come. You will come to me on that day. Trust, trust, trust.

Tell of my Word, but do not be discouraged when some turn away. Live for Me and those who are dear to you. Keep My Word.

Why? Why? Why, Lord?

Something upsetting is happening, so I rush to You in prayer. Feeling frustrated, I ask, "Holy Spirit, will You come forth so I can know You?"

And He says:

I am in you now. I come forth in a river of love from your eyes. You do not have to see Me to know of My presence. Even though I am within you, I will still lead you as if I were in front of you. Now watch Me closely, and carefully follow My way.

Impulsive tendencies that men have will soon melt away when I am left in control. I do not ask this of you, but I insist upon it, as you have already promised to obey Me. Stop wailing in front of Me, and start praying to Me for your petitions. As always, they are in the hands of Jesus Christ, who will do all things necessary according to His will. You must learn to be sensitive to Me, for I, the Holy Spirit, am sensitive. Loudness and rashness are annoying to Me.

Praise to God the Father, God the Son, and God the Holy Spirit in Jesus' name. Amen.

Trust

(John 6:37)

I cried, *"Lord, help me. Where are you? I need you!"*

And He says:

The river from which you cry is not from Me, but from frustration (see 1 John 2:23-25). Your tears are not of the Spirit, but pain in your flesh. Look not to what hurts you, but look to the One who fulfills you. I will take away your pain when you rest in Me. You must trust in Me; otherwise you will become tempted to do the enemy's will. I will not have this in My house.

Go to the children and show them My love through you; they must see this sign for their salvation. You ask if they are saved, but I tell you that unless a man bears the fruit of his Master, he is not. If My children will not listen, but instead let the evil one have his way with them, they cannot come with Me on that glorious day. But they will remain and suffer much heartache because they did not heed My Word. They must be made aware of My love. You must do this for me—you must.

The time is short, and while everyone is busy gathering the lustful things of this world, My Father's Word is being fulfilled as it has been written. Many will be left behind for lack of knowledge, and many will perish.

The eternity that you know of in your heart is real, and the eternity My Father has provided for the evil one is real also. My Father will not be mocked nor ridiculed, and as it has been written,

"No one will come to the Father but through Me."

I tell you, My child, much will be written about Me, but only those who have Me in their heart will know Me. Dry your eyes, My child, for much goodness is to come. Trust in Me, the Lord your God, and all things I have promised you will come to pass.

Come Closer

Look not at the material things I gave you, but look toward your center, My Spirit, which rests in your heart. All these things I have given you, but you still look to the material. Wake up, My child, focus on Me; pay attention to every detail of Me, for I am always talking with you. Tune Me in; tune out the world. In this way you will do all that is right while you are still in the world. I will continue to tell you of things now and for all time. It is difficult to hear My voice when you are crying about earthly things.

Put your emotions behind your love for Me. You can use them, but only after you know My will. Then, together with the knowledge I give you, you will act in a complete way. I am always looking for obedience in My children, but many fall short. But you—I talk to you. You do My work, and I, the Lord, smile upon you and bless you.

Your blessings will come in many ways: some

earthly, some spiritual. Whatever happens to you or your family, there is a blessing from Me. Accept My blessing and remember to always be thankful. Do not worry about who is with Me or who is against Me, for I know all things and only I will judge. Those who do not wish to hear of My ways are taking their rewards on earth.

I will build you a fine house. It is to be for the children and your family, and it will be a house filled with an abundance of love. Do not be concerned about when or where, because all things will be in My time. Do you understand? Continue to discuss all things with your spouse, and wait for the time when all things will be made clear to you. Do not hurry in your decisions, for that will *surely* bring despair. Trust in Me, My child, for I am your Father, and I will see that all good things come to you. I know you have many questions, but you must be patient. Do not let Satan steal anything from you, and remember what I told you concerning him.

Learn to move slowly in your decisions so that I may speak with you *first* in all matters! Sometimes you must let go of the obvious. Hold onto your faith, for only through faith will all things be given to you. Go along now and remember to be kind to all for My name's sake.

Forgiven

Precious Lord, forgive me: I am still learning,
and I act out of Your will many times. I want to be
reconciled with You in spite of the wrong I have
done. What must I do to feel your closeness again? I
miss you so. . . .

And He says:

Carry not your burden so heavy, but lean on
Me, for I am your rock and your salvation. I will
lift you up and make you whole. I see your repentance, and you are worthy of forgiveness for
that which you have done against Me. My child,
how else must you learn, if not by your mistakes?
I love you and wait for you in the darkest of your
tribulations.

Don't you see how I am? I am wholly
forgiving. While your Spirit is broken, My Spirit
sings for joy, for blessed is the Lord at all times.
You do not know Me or My ways as you think
you do, for only the Father knows. Take only
what I give you, as gifts, and do not assume on
Me, for then I will surely turn away. I would turn
away for your good; otherwise you might think
your will is My will; but that will never be.

Breathe in My Spirit, My sweet child: It's
over now. Come back into My grace, and there I
will shine upon you. You need not fall away in
times of trouble, but instead you must hold on. I

30

tell you again: I am your rock. Do not be afraid to fasten yourself to Me so that you may not be moved. I am with you always, but you must be brought into line if you expect a high place with Me in My house.

Your spirit has been made to bend and break and fall, but Mine is never-changing. This is how you learn! Do you understand? My peace is with you, for you have taken your heartache to My feet in sorrow. I love you, dear precious child of My Father.

3
GOD THE ENCOURAGER

He Understands

(2 Timothy 1:7)

I inquired of the Lord, and He heard my cry.

What is it, My child, that makes you weep? Do you think that I do not understand? Come and rest beside Me for awhile, and I will ease your pain. Hush and be still: I want to talk with you. Do not be so caught up with feelings; they are to be used to express yourself, not to destroy you. Do not become unnecessarily burdened. There is nothing you can do to change the heart of the one who hurts you. But I understand, because I love you with the love you would have for a child struggling to walk. How your heart goes out to that little one, but you must let him go and stumble over and over again. It is like that with Me: Each time I must let you go your own way so that you might grow and learn.

You still depend greatly on those in the world

to give you inward satisfaction. You do need others in your life, but only I can understand your heart! So today, when you are feeling misunderstood, I want you to know that I understand every feeling in you. Be strong and courageous, knowing I am at your side, for I did not give you a spirit of timidity, but a spirit of strength! Take more time for yourself and do not feel guilty for doing so, because you need quiet time to be alone with Me. While inwardly you hurt right now, you must remember that you live by the promise I have given you. And when that promise becomes reality, you will never cry again.

But for now, I have left you with hope. You did not have this hope before you knew Me. That hope will see you through if you do not grow weary. Your life is no longer your own because you have willingly submitted it to Me. I will see you through. Call on the "name above all names," for He is wonderful, and it is only because of Him that you have hope. See, I have made a way.

Little Child

Do not worry if you will be here or there. I tell you that you will be with Me on that glorious day and for all time. What does it matter where you are now, if you keep Me in your heart? Do you understand?

My child, you are so precious to Me that I will tell you of good things to come. Things in your life will change, but I will never change; I will always be exactly the same. But you will come to know Me better as you learn to pray and talk with Me.

Do not be concerned with life's problems as you see them, but do be concerned with all things that are of Me. I will lead you to special places and tell you of spectacular things that men do not know, but only the Father knows. You will see as you let yourself go in My arms. I will rock you and comfort you when you are weary and lonely. I will be your shield against any harm that may come toward you. I will protect you at all times, if you will only trust and believe in Me.

All that I have for you will make you smile, because I know of love and good things, if only you will ask. When you talk to Me, it is like a prayer. It makes Me happy. When I am happy, you will be happy, because we are sharing the blessing of our Father in heaven.

So you see, My sweet child, all things will be made perfect for you, because I will never leave you. You can go away from Me because of your will; but even then, when things go wrong, you need only say, "Jesus, help me," and I will be at your side. Remember always that you are as important to Me as the most honored person in heaven, because you carry My Spirit within you. Be strong, sweet one: I, Jesus, have a crown for you. Won't you walk with Me?

I'm Your Answer

Lord Jesus, help me. My Jesus, I need You.
My Jesus, my Jesus, help me.

Do you think I'm not there?
Do you worry in care?
Do you honestly trust Me? Do you?
If we are as one, do *you* say that we are?
If it's true, then I'm crying with you.
If your heart aches, I see,
and My finger touches your tears.
Don't be sad in this time: I will make you a way.
Come and follow My lead; you will see.
Don't be quick to give up—it's not over yet!
You don't know what the outcome will be.
If you'll just take My hand and
Trust in My time,
I will give you your heart's desire.
Put away now your tears, dry your eyes,
and look up to Me: I'm your answer.

35

Do you hear what I say? Is it clear to you now?
I'm your answer—I'm your answer.
Is it deep in your ear, reaching your soul?
I'm your answer—I'm your answer.
I'M YOUR ANSWER!
So rest in Me: I will comfort you.
I long to show you My ways.
You need not be heavy, when I am light.
Don't you know I'll always be there?
I will make your path straight,
and I'll support you;
holding you with My strength.
Don't you know? Don't you know it?
Rest assured. Rest assured.
These things in the world will come
now and then.
But I tell you: do not fear.
For if I am the vine and you are a branch,
why would you worry at all?
Where is your faith? Where is your faith?
By now you're beginning to see that
it's just one hour at a time, trusting in Me—
just one day walking in Me.
Drink from the vine and fill yourself.
Don't be tense, for the waters won't flow.
Just relax, take a breath, and settle down.
Breathe Me in and drink from My cup.
Come flow with Me;
Come bend with Me in the river.

Come in deeper—come in deeper!
Now look down upon yourself; what do you see?
My water has covered you.
Now *you* can't see yourself—
only *My reflection,*
as the water becomes a mirror of Me.
Don't you see? Don't you see how *you* are?
Why trouble yourself with the world?
As I look after you, so I look after them,
for everything is in My hand.
Now you understand that I'm your answer!
Now you understand what you need.

The Birthday

The eyes of the Lord are upon me: I cannot hide. Your presence overwhelms me. I want not to write, but to be alone with you and taken into rest. But You say, "Write." Why must I do this when I want to rest?

And He says:

My child, you are tired and overburdened. To take refuge in Me is not work. You try so hard, so afraid to make a mistake. Am I so harsh that I would not understand? Stop trying to do things to please Me, for that is not what I want. I have many angels who please Me always. I wish to talk with you. I wish to know how you feel about the earth which is around you. What do you like? Do you like the color of the sky? Is it too blue? The grass in the field—what do you think about it? I will always supply all your needs, but that is not why I chose you to be. I chose you to be so I might walk with you. I chose you to be so you might love Me.

Today is the day you were born. Today is your birthday. Will you celebrate it with your Father? Today is a day of joy. I love you so much. Look at all you have. Have I not always provided for you? Be content this day, for there will not be another one like it. Here are words of wisdom on this, your birthday: First know the Truth and rest in it, for you cannot find rest in what you do not know.

> Happy Birthday, My Beloved.
> Your Father

Encouragement

You are spirit first; then you are flesh.
Jesus is My heart, poured out for you.
I am, and will remain in you for as long as you will have Me. My beloved, look how you are; you are not in rags as you see yourself.

Look! I have dressed you in splendor. Rejoice and be glad, for I have made this day for you and put all things under your feet—yes, even yours.

You can wait a little longer, for all those things I have written about in My Word will come to pass. There is so much to be done to prepare for that day.

Look now how your hands have become skillful. You must continue for the sake of truth. Have I not made you prosper? Have you not grown? Have you not increased? Have courage; be strong in Christ. Do not become complacent, and do not give way to weariness, for I will lift you, *says the Spirit of the Lord*. Look at Me now: I am all, together, and am One. Come.

Take Heart

Surely I am with you, says the Spirit of the Lord. I see your distress, and I have sent My angels to comfort you. Do not let your heart be troubled when the ways of men disappoint you. I have put you here to call on Me for your every need; to receive healing from Me; and in your thankfulness, to worship Me.

When life seems to have no purpose, at these times, I will remind you of My promise: If you will give back to Me the very thing I have given to you, you will reap the rewards of heaven, and you will no longer cry. But in this life there will be challenging times like this. It is important that you understand the frailty of humanity, and choose the Spirit and His realm to walk in.

The Mirror

Look in the mirror. What do you see?

I see myself as I am, and I am not worthy. I just see myself.

Do you see yourself as you really are, or do you see an image of yourself?

I see an image of myself, but an image is only image.

You are not really seeing yourself. An image reveals how *you* visualize yourself to be. But an image is not real, but only that which you perceive. Look in the mirror again, but this time look beyond the image, look into what creates the image.

Yes, you have created the image. Look at the blood that flows through you. Look at your body within: Look at your heart and now seek your soul, for there lies your real self. Keep focusing beyond the mirror, and you will sense your spirit. Bathe in the beauty of it. For *this* is what the Lord has given you. *This* is who you are.

It's All Right If You Don't Answer

Holy Spirit, tell me about life. Why do I always mess up? Why do I continue to make the wrong choices? Why does life have to be such an obstacle course? I already know that what I say is most of the problem. This is not fun, Lord. Will I ever get it right? Hardly not, I feel! I want you to talk with Me so I can know and understand how You feel about these things. There are so many things I do wrong. As I grow in You, I thought it would get smoother; but no, I just encounter different circumstances. I feel better already; at least it's on paper and not still boggling my mind.

It's all right if You do not answer.

And He says:

Child, what are you doing to yourself? Are you that aggravated with life in the world? Have I given you too much? Come closer and lend your ear to the instruction of your Father. These things that are happening are not overpowering; each in itself has little ability to set you back. Why do you look at them all at once, instead of finding time to come alone to Me with each one? I am a Father of detail, but yet you wait until you become as an overloaded paintbrush which cannot define the things it wishes to express.

Come to Me with the little you have; you are not sparing Me by waiting and bringing a full load to Me. Once again, I bring to you the word *simplicity*. You do not have to take a stand on everything that passes by you, do you? Be still more often and observe. This way will take understanding, discernment and wisdom. This path is not difficult. I am teaching you right now, using the simplest of instruction.

To answer all of your questions, I say to you: learn to rest while you are awake! Do you realize that everything you have asked Me comes from your anxious heart? In this world mistakes will always be made, but they can be greatly minimized if you will walk in rest more than you do. Stop being so concerned about everyone, because in your own strength you are not going to make that much of a difference. Only I can change a heart, and only through prayer and petition will you truly understand grace.

In all your mistakes and in all your wrong choices, you continually underestimate the power of My grace, which is all-sufficient. I have answered all of your questions except for one. It is not for Me to tell you about life; it is for you to experience life through Me and understand that the source of life is *in* Me. Because of My

Beloved Son, the Christ, you have been given life, even more abundantly. Certain things I have put in your path so that you will grow. Other things are obstacles that are not for you to contend with. Let My peace and good cheer mend you today. Be concerned with only what is necessary. Just ask yourself as you go along each day and problems arise, *Is it necessary for me to get involved?* In your new understanding, you will see a difference.

My child, you can come to Me anytime with anything. Remember, *I* am your Father.

———◆———

A Sense of Falseness

Why are you afraid to speak what is in your heart? The Spirit within you holds the truth. That which is true is held by the believer in his heart, but are you afraid to speak it? I have put the truth within you, and you shall speak it as you are obedient to the Father. It is not true that you are out of order when you must speak the truth. Are you not a temple for the Lord Most High? If you abide in Me and I in you, there is no fear of condemnation. You cannot be condemned when you speak the truth.

———◆———

Rock and Fortress

Lord, You will not be moved; if I am in You, neither shall I be moved.

These things the Lord says:

To be fruitful, one must sow; to reap, one must have first worked. How can you take from Me what you have not yet earned? I tell you the truth, unless a man be true to Me in his spirit, I shall not hear him. You say you want and you need; you put yourself first, your desires next, then Me. I will not have this. But I promise you a crown, if only you will become obedient to My Father.

Don't you see, little one, how much your Father loves you? Don't you see that perfect love cannot exist without discipline? You are being trained for a mighty work. These things I cannot allow you to be: prideful, boastful, conceited, anxious, petty and unforgiving. Turn loose your wicked ways, and come follow Me. I have life for you in abundance. Won't you hear My voice? Won't you let Me lead? Won't you allow My Spirit to become your guide? If you do these things, you will surely have a mansion in My house.

Come now, child, put away your childish games and come with Me, for I am your strength and the source of all things. What must I do to have you open your ears and silence your stubbornness? I must allow you to stumble, to feel pain, and to grow. A life with Me will not be easy, as you know, for truly you will be persecuted because of your belief in Me. But if you will endure, I promise you a life of splendor and of beauty beyond what you can know.

My dear child, I do not reprimand you because you are not good. No, I do it because you are most precious in My sight. Your place is with Me in My house.

Breaking Forth

Behold, I am alive within you. I live within you. My Spirit has been captured deep within you. I have filled you with My Spirit deep within the depths of your body. I am there. I am alive. I am made alive in you by the power of My Spirit.

So, you have done this thing that has been your desire for so long. How beautiful a moment it is when My child shares what his Father has made the world from—My Spirit.

Now, My child, this is how you pray:

Father, I adore you.
Father, I love you.
Father, you are blessed in my sight.
I kneel before You in Your majesty.
I glorify Your Name in all I do.

Precious Spirit, surround me, encompass me, and hold me. I glorify Your Name, my Maker, my King. Jesus, yes, you live within me now. I worship and adore You; I kneel at Your feet. I give You praise and I thank You for dying for Me. I will allow You the freedom to work through me. Your will be done in this temple that is mine. My entire temple is all of me, and it is filled with You alone. Magnify Yourself within me and release Your power through every part of me. Now this has become my prayer, Lord, and my song—a song written by You, and for You.

Just the Beginning
(Philippians 4:13; 2 Corinthians 1:22;
Psalms 1:3)

Look how you are. Really look. Do you see the light of the Lord shine through your face? Do you see His work, His finished work? What do you see? For you are yet but a child. I will build you. You will do great things for Me, and I will grow you and bless you. I will make you Mine, and you will make Me yours. I love you with a love you have never known; My love is pure, unlike any you have known.

I watch you always, and I search your heart to pull forth all that is good and to lay waste to all that is not of Me. You have just barely touched the beginning of understanding as I would have you understand. Do not be afraid to go up against the one who wants to steal that which I have given you. I have equipped you with a spirit that can do all things through Christ, who has been given to you as a deposit, which ensures your future forever. Do you understand? Are you too young? No, you are not.

Take these words of wisdom and sow them unto yourself, so you may have power to fight the battle. These things that you know now are nothing compared to what I am going to show you. You will see; and it will not be when you are old, but while you are still young! I search with My eyes for those who will bring in *the end time harvest*. Are you interested? It will not be easy, but if you choose to follow Me, I will equip you with everything you need. I will supply all your needs. I will plant you by the water where you will never grow weary.

My child, I hold out My hand to you. What will you do?

4
GOD'S CHURCH:
HIS CALL TO ATTENTION

Hear What I Say

For the few that believe—for the few that *really* believe—let them be made known. In hardship, you will know who they are. For they will be sustained, as if tied to the Rock. Oh, there is a mighty day coming, and My people must be prepared. I have already told you about this day.

I see your heart cry out to Me for answers and there seem to be none coming. But wait—I have not forgotten you. In these times, I am revealing Myself to you in ways you have not as yet known.

Pray for revelation and pray for joy, for in the midst of these two, I am there in strength and in wisdom to aid you against the enemy. I will show you by My Spirit how to command the enemy. I will teach you how to precisely use the Word to seek and occupy what has been yours all along. Do not give up and do not be fainthearted, for I am with you, says the Lord of Hosts. Trust Me and do as I say, and you will see victory.

———◆◆———

Write the Vision

What should I write, Lord? I don't see anything.

Don't write what you see; write what I see. Write what I have called forth from the beginning. Write the things of simpleness and pureness of the heart—write of My desire. You are unable to see as I do, yet you are hungry for My lost as I am; and without understanding, you desire to win for Me that which I long for.

My Church, My Church, I have made you for Myself—to clothe you, to partake with you, and to reveal you unto Myself in glory; to stir up within you the call to serve, so that I may in turn serve you. You are My delight, My crown and My glory, and without you there is no vision. I have purposed you and fashioned you from the depths of what I am. I am that "I am" in you; am I not?

Look not to the world for its beauty in all that I have made, for that is only for a time. But look to them who are eternal beings, whose inward beauty waits to be revealed.

You! I have called *you* to reveal Myself to

them! I want all of what is Mine to return to Me from whence they came; by choice, not by persuasion and not be force, but by an open heart—by emptiness and loneliness. The lonely, the suffering, those who are unable and those who are bound: They are My treasures. They are My beloved. My vision is to share life with them and to bring them into My bosom.

Now that I have revealed My vision to you, will you partake in it? Will you do the work of a laborer? Will you devote the life you now have to bring it to birth? Can I count you in as one who will serve? Reach them, teach them, and touch them by the power I have given you because of the Light who came to you. Do not think about your reward, for *in no way* can you comprehend it.

It is for the vision that you live and I *am* the vision. I am the desire and I am the reality. I am.

The Cost

I have not called for a church of riches; I have called for a church of *value,* says the Spirit of the Lord. Have I not told you that I would pour out My Spirit on all mankind? Have I not promised this? What are you doing counting the change in your pocket, when I have given you the riches of heaven? I reproach you, for your ways are of waste before Me. I will tear down, says the Spirit of the Lord. I will tear it all down.

Hurry while there is still time and receive reproof, for I am coming, and I will burn up the chaff. If you intend to stand on that day, you must lay aside *all* of your ways—I have need for none of them. If you cannot stand pure before Me, then I cannot be in your presence. I will not know you because I will not be able to see you. Do you understand? I cannot see you! I want you, My Church, but you must allow yourself to be perfected—and yes, it will cause you great human pain. But if you will withstand My breath of purification, *then* I will come for you as a bridegroom reaching out for the hand of his beloved.

How I love you, My people. How I love you!

Who Will?
(Isaiah 6:8)

Would you not touch the hand of a leper? Are you so clean, having no filth? Lo, I say unto you this day, unless a man be willing to lay down his life for his brother, he is not worthy of Me, and he has no love in him. Those who are coming, those behind the flood gates, are sick, and many will not be acceptable in your eyes. What will you do? Who will help and who will serve now that the birthing has begun? Oh, but did you expect beauty after all the pain? Did you expect a garden? Look at My people. Look past what you see with your natural eyes, and see into the faces of those whom I love and cherish! Will you continue to run the race, or will you too become tempted to sit by the wayside and rest?

This is a time like none other, and I will not alter what has been predestined to be. I will not hold back the floodgates for you to get prepared. Either you are ready, or you will say, "No." Give Me your answer! Sound the alarm! The need is great. Where are the workers? Who will say, "Yes, here I am?"

He who has the Spirit in him has the Father, and he who has the Father also knows the Son.

Be Aware

On that glorious day, the angels and saints will say, "Amen, Amen." That day shall be glorious to some, but agonizing to others. For they who do not know Me will be lost forever.

To you who have faith, more will be given. For My flock will increase abundantly. Many, many will come—even those who are asleep and do not yet know Me.

They will come with tears,

They will come with joy,
They will come with burdens,
They will come with sins,
They will come with thirst,
They will come with hunger,
They will come with lies,
They will come with unforgiveness,
They will come with pain,
They will come with anguish,
They will come with fornication,
They will come with sorrow,
They will come full,
They will come hungry,
They will come clothed,
They will come unclothed,
They will come in all walks of life,
They will come from different ways,
But they will come.

Hurry now, My children, hurry; for your home is with Me, where you will be safe from what is to be. Gather up what is important for your salvation, and leave behind the rest!

I tell you *beware,* for you do not know the power of Satan. But from behind Me, he has no power. *Do you see* where you must be? I offer only love and a city of glory for all who ask.

Won't you receive?

New Breed Church

Today I have set Myself against some, in order that they might repent. For they have done evil in My sight.

These things have not been hidden from My eye, though men think I do not see. I will cause a flood to come upon them, and then they will know I am the Lord. For Mine is not to avenge, but to save. But if My people will not listen, they will surely perish. I will take them out, unless they turn from their evil ways.

I am stirring up a new breed. They will be stronger and mightier than those who walked before them, for they are bringing the news of salvation and love as never before, and I am equipping them so that they will be heard.

No longer will they reach deaf ears; no longer will they not be seen. For those I am sending are a new breed that *will* be seen and heard. Those who are held captive will be given another chance to receive Me, but the time grows short, and many will be lost. But I, the Lord, will bring about justice in this land, and you will see and know that what I have said will come to pass.

Wake Up

I am looking for a people. I am looking for a people who will serve Me with reverence in their hearts. I do not desire their words of praise which come forth out of unclean hearts; I will not receive from impureness. I have called My people to be holy. "Holy" means without inward desire to go against what I desire: My commandment of love—for I am love. And if I reside within My people, they must worship Me *out of love*.

I hear in My ear, "How I desire Your presence, oh my Lord," but I will not give it to them, because they do not reverence My name. My name is *holy*. When you call on My name, you also must *be* holy; otherwise there can be no communication.

Hear what I say, churches, because the time draws near. Pay attention to what you are doing! Lay flat your own hearts and examine them. See to it that there are no lumps. Work them out—all of them. I tell you if you are not willing to listen, you will miss Me. You will not see Me at all!

Yes, I love you. I hunger for you to be with Me, but I will not have a tainted Church, because I am pure—I cannot, because I will not divide what I am. I could not do it for My only Son, and I will not do it for you. I call you to be a people who will understand holiness and its properties. It is not difficult; you *think* it is, but it is not.

You are full of the world, and you are blinded! Bow down so you can see Me. For the lower you become before Me, the higher I will take you in Me. Are you beginning to understand? I am not harsh, but you must be able to withstand correction, and then do the very thing, properly, that you were corrected for. Come away from yourself. Let Me show you a better way and a better life, for My concern is that you *live*.

Wake up, My people, and wipe the slumber from your eyes. Otherwise, you will forever sleep in darkness.

For Such a Time

Oh Lord, what's wrong? Everything seems confusing and unclear. I want so much to be strongly focused on You, but it is like there are missiles flying in the air, at home and everywhere I go. Things are not running smoothly. Just when it looks like things are going to be all right, suddenly they start turning upside down. What is happening? It's getting worse. I will continue to hold onto you, but I'm losing understanding of the people and circumstances around me.

And the Spirit of the Lord says:

Blessed are those who have a watchful eye, for they shall determine the times. These are times like never before and there will not be a rest in them before the end, and it will not be prolonged. Why do you hesitate when I call you to Myself? I call you to pray, but you find things to fuss with instead. I am gathering My children to Myself because the times are near and I do not want any to be lost. You must remain close to Me; otherwise, you will miss the sound of My voice. Come closer to Me now, for this will be a time like never before. Be inseparable from My Spirit who speaks with you—let no one come between us.

What you are feeling is the beginning of *the great separation* of those who are with Me and those who *say* they are.

A Message of Preparation

Do not be deceived, for great is the deception of the world. Stand forthright in all that you do, and do not compromise. I tell you the truth this day. Many who say they believe, do not!

Do not be alarmed by these things, for they must happen: When you see a brother embrace another while there is hatred yet in his heart, fear not. Even when you see these things in your own church—oh yes—know that I am there in your midst. I am there.

This is a time of great testing. Many are being tested who feel *they* have no need to be tested. They say they are true, but they deceive themselves!

Happy are those who cling to My love—they are the ones who will surely inherit My kingdom! Yes, I said My kingdom is yours: you who are upright, you who witness to the truth by the example of your lives.

Do not worry about those who will receive and who will not receive, for you cannot know these things; but only the Father knows. My peace I leave with you as an assurance of what is to come.

The excitement has already begun in heaven for that which is to come! Be ready by being made ready.

My Churches Are Divided

You come in My name, and all of you come to Me and My Father. You are torn between the teaching of man and My words. Did I tell you to follow Me? Did I tell you to walk as I do? Did I tell you to teach My ways? Did I tell you that you are to come to Me?

You are of Me, and I am *in* you. Why is there so much strife within you? Are there not enough wars to be fought? Must any more be fought among you because of My name? I will tell you—don't do this! Unite and be set free in Me.

For only through Me can you really be free. But through your differences, you will remain in bondage, and because of that, many will not know Me—only *of* Me. Do you see what the evil one does to you? He causes division in those who belong to Me. Better to trust in Me for one moment than to be led by evil throughout eternity. Do you understand? You can know the truth in one moment by *asking* for Me, for only through Me will you be able to know. *Then* your eternity will be with My Father in heaven, and you will wear a glorious crown.

Oh My people, come together quickly. Do not divide over man's rules. Time is short; you must listen. There is room for all in My house.

———◆◆◆———

I Need a People

Write. These things I say to you today:

I watch you and I see your works.

I see your humbleness before Me.

I see the breaking within you.

I see your repentance before Me.

I am pleased.

I see your great fear of Me. It is right to fear Me, for I am all-powerful.

I see you in your brokenness and your inability to approach My throne, as if a mighty wind were against you. Do not fear Me in that way, for I want you to come closer.

I am before you. Stand straight and come.

I want to bless you today for what you have done through the Spirit of Christ within you.

Today, you allowed Me to have complete authority so that My work could be completed. The evil of this world is Mine to avenge. I will pull down the strongman who lays siege to that which belongs to My children. Today, you have allowed Me to do that through you.

Man's selfish ways are not My ways. There is nothing man can do for Me on his own—not one thing—for man does not possess the wisdom of God; but *only I.*

Now today you see that you have the victory, but who fought the battle? Was it you? What did you have to do with it? Do you see how men hinder My ways? I will take out the enemy, if you will allow My Spirit to rise up within you and take full control. For I am the Master, and I hold the wheel of the ship. How simple it is for you to understand now. Do not try to figure what your Father will do, for you cannot know.

I want My people to be available to Me at all times, for time, as you know it, is short. There is still much to be done. I need My people to be willing! I need them to put off the self of this world and yield themselves to the call of My Spirit!

Tell them not to hold resentment for one another; tell them to love and not hate; and tell them to no longer be selfish. Even when they pray in the Spirit, they are selfish. I need a people I can work through. I need those who will become empty of their worldly ways.

I ache with love for you, My people. I made you for Myself so that I *could* love you. I have so much to give you. I am your Father and I love you! Listen to My voice. Do as I say; do not question My ways. Be obedient, be kind, have mercy, and above all, be forgiving. For in forgiveness comes love; in love comes patience; and in patience, understanding.

Tell them—tell all who will listen! Tell them that I will supply *all* their needs, just as I did in times of old. Tell them to put aside their ways and follow the way of Jesus Christ, My Son. If only they knew of the banquet being prepared for them, surely they would listen!

Today, My child, I thank you.

No Time for Joking

I have set My Spirit to dancing among you. Will you not receive the spirit of joy? Will you not allow yourselves to become engulfed in My presence? Lo, I say unto you now, if you will not receive what I am sending you, how do you intend to tarry? Many of you are looking for a free ride. I *will* take you up with me, but only if you diligently seek Me. I am not present for one moment and gone the next. I am *continually* pouring out Myself on all who will receive. I ache with love for you, My people!

Look closely at yourselves and one another; what do you see? What are your actions, and how do you present yourselves? I am a loving and kind God; but I will not allow My temple to be defiled. And if I must move away from you in order to bring about My will, then I *will* move from you.

These are not times for joking and merriment, but times for battle! The time draws nearer, and I must have a people who are prepared. No longer will I tolerate complacency among you; but I will now require militant and steadfast unity between you for one cause—to bring in *the harvest* which is against the floodgates. Do you hear Me? Do you care? What must I do so that you might have a hearing ear? Those of you who wish to be counted say, "Amen." For I will not wait any longer for you to *state* your position and then *act* upon it.

The angels in heaven rejoice with your Lord

and Savior, Jesus Christ, and they all say, "Amen."

To the Church

You have been called to pray—not play.

You have been called to sacrifice—not socialize.

You have been called out of darkness—not into death.

Consider everything in prayer—not feelings.

Hold fast to the Word—not to each other. *Now* is not a time to sleep; *now* is not a time to rest. This is a time of battle. NOW!

Wake up. Do you not hear the trumpet's blast? Are you so deaf? What are you doing? You are not prepared, and the battle has already begun! I have called you and continue to call you to be a people of prayer, because this battle will be won through, and only through, diligent prayer. I have called you! I have called you! Will you not get up and do the things I have set for you to do? Do not be deceived; let no one deceive you. Disengage yourself from the enemy's hands. Do not become ensnared in anything he does, for he comes to provoke you and tantalize you, and you may become curious. Be curious only to observe the spirit, and then to test it to see if it is of good or evil. If the spirit is not of Me, run from it. Run quickly and do not look back, otherwise it will tempt you again. Like a lion who tears at its prey, so will he tear at you—stay away from everything that is not of Me!

My commandments are your guideline; use them every day. You must continue to put them into practice so that you will not be shaken in *this time* of war. I have given My angels charge over you, but they can do nothing if you will not yield and be willing to take instruction. Do you understand? Gird yourself, My people. Prepare for war, for the battle has already begun. Reach out in the Spirit and go forth and take down spiritual strongholds that the enemy has set up.

Tear them down in your home,

Tear them down in your work,

Tear them down in the schools,

Tear them down in the cities,

Tear them down in the government,

Tear them down in the world.

Don't fight this battle with anger, but with *joy,* for I have equipped you for victory! Through the power of the shed blood of Jesus Christ, you are able to walk in perfect liberty. Do not try to fight with any part of yourself, or you will become frustrated. Fight only by My Spirit, which I have placed in you—*then* you will fight as a mighty warrior of valor! I will show you each move, step by step, and you will maneuver with grace and precision, and *nothing* will stop you! Yes, this is truly a joyful time! My people are coming together all over the world; they are uniting as one in prayer as they force their way through the heavenly realms.

◆ ◆ ◆

See What I See

And the Spirit of the Lord says:

Look not to man, for he is there for only a moment in time. I have set My Spirit free to mingle among the people—am I not everywhere? Do My eyes not see all? Surely you recognize Me when I am present among you. I watch you sing, and I see you praise; but who among you will mock Me? I go forth in pureness and sweetness, but many receive with a haughty spirit—yes, even many where you are.

I will shake My churches, and during that time, you will say it is dry and that the Spirit is not moving in this place. Look how quickly they are discouraged. Look how quickly they move to another place in hopes of being fed. This is nothing new. Are you also so anxious to move on, or will you wait and see a new thing? I will move on that church, and I will *preserve* all who are willing to persevere and not grow weary. My power will be as strong for two as for 22. You look at everything in numbers, but I do not. I look only at the heart, and I am looking for a people who will keep a pure heart.

Do not become impatient, for the hand of the Lord is moving over the top of the building, and you will see a new thing! Do not put stock in what your *eyes* see. You will see what I am doing if you will hold steadfast onto the truth. How long will you stay? Will you leave when there are 10 left? How many?

This is what I tell you, and it will be good if you share this: Many will come near the end, and they will cry, "Let me in! Help me," but that will only be the beginning! They will be like those with gnashing of teeth; they will be the outcasts of their own people and families. There will be much pain and crying, and many will run from them, but they are My people, and I will send them to *those places* where I know they will be received.

If you want to go, go now, for I tell you these things will happen! My people are hurt, diseased and dying; they are decrepit among men. Many will fear them—*even* those I call My own—those who have done a mighty work for My kingdom!

So, I am not taking away from your church—I am building it. Many will not understand, and many will ridicule; but I tell you that those who will not be moved and continue to remain will receive a double portion of the anointing which is to come. So now I tell this church to continue, to go forward, to make new plans, to not feel faint, to disregard pressure, and to hold onto the absolute, which is the truth as you know it through Jesus Christ.

Do not be saddened when you see some leave, but rejoice, for the time draws nearer. There will be a reward for enduring all this, but who among you can remain now that the shaking has begun?

To the Church

(John 3:16)

I sat at my table weeping because of the blindness of the saints of God—those who have been endowed with power, but refuse to act out in it according to the Word of God. They forget that God so loved the world that He gave. . . .

And the Spirit of the Lord says:
Write, I say to you. Write, for the time draws

nearer, and many will be lost. These will be times like never before, and only a few will stand. The Church is lazy, and she is stupid, because she thinks I will carry her off in a loving embrace. But I will not, says the Spirit of the Lord, for they will not come! I have come to them night after night, but they will not wake from their slumber. They hear Me, and they know that it is I; but they do not pay attention to My voice, and they sleep and they sleep.

A time is coming when there will be no rest; and in that time, they will look for Me, but it will be *too late,* for I will have already gone with those who were one with Me.

You see: Now is the time of the Church who speaks My name and does wonders *in* My name, but many are not one with Me because of sin they refuse to come away from. They are so *deluded* that they have covered over their sin, and they no longer even *see* it! They praise My name and say, "The Lord is good"; but it will *not* be good for them on that day when I come!

Bewitched

You are bewitched, My people whom I love. You are trading your crown of glory for a lie. The enemy came like sweet honey to you, and you ate of it. I am grieved because I had warned you, and still you disobeyed Me, *says the Spirit of the Lord*. Not only did you not listen to Me, but you also have taken *My* precepts and shaped them into *your* precepts. Now you are deceived. Now your eyes are cast over, and you are unable to see My calling for holiness.

Look at your hands: Can you stand before Me and say to Me that they have not defiled Me? Your words do not persuade Me, neither do your offerings; they are as empty baskets, empty because they are filled with your deceptive deeds! Nevertheless, I cry out to you; nevertheless, I hunger for you; nevertheless, I love you. I lament with a sobbing heart because of My deep love for you. I do not intend to cast you aside, but to chasten you so that you might heed correction. My way is not to alienate you, but to woo you.

Have you not discerned the times, and have you not considered the words of My prophets? Why do you continually try to smooth out the wrinkles in *your* garment, when I have set before you a garment of righteousness? You are caught up in the surface when I have called you to the *deep*. If you will not come *deep*, you will eventually perish. I know the things that you do not know, but yet you trifle with Me.

I wish for you to consider Martha and Mary. Though they both loved Me, only Mary identified with My heart, while Martha did not understand. Martha was blinded by the things of the surface, while Mary was concerned with the things of the deep. Heed My words, Church; hear them, and do not delay in seeking wisdom. The thoughts of your soul are like dust in the wind: You think you do good, and you gather with others to think about doing good, but you are missing the *mark,* and you toil in vain!

Have I not called you, My people, to be in Me, with Me, and by Me, through prayer and petition? If I am what you really want, as you declare, then you must change—change your soulful prayers and pray only by My leading; otherwise, you pray amiss! You *are* listening now, but for how long? I am coming with a vengeance to gather up what is Mine—those who are truly faithful—and I will leave behind many whom I deeply love. I implore you to consider your ways and ask you to walk away from the garment that defiles you.

Like a corrupt government, My people are going further and further astray by the leading of bewitching spirits—they have put a haze over your eyes. Break away while there is still time and cleanse yourself, for I cannot place My garment over that which is defiled.

Yes, I come after My sheep when they go astray, but there will come a time when the door will be closed.

Wake Up, Warrior

It's 2:45 A.M. Everything in me says, "Go back to bed." So why am I up? Is it Your presence I feel, or is it my mind playing tricks on me? I'm tired, yet awake. If there is a reason why I'm sitting here, God, will You please let me know what it is?

And He says:

I hear You call yourself a warrior and an intercessor, but yet you have trouble putting on your armor in the middle of the night. The enemy troops are advancing while you sleep. Wake from your slumber and back them off. Don't you see there is no set time to fight? We war day and night against the principalities in high places.

Yes, you have a warring spirit, but you are lax about the things of battle. First, above all things, you must be ready at all times—not only when you *choose* to pray. Second, the fitting of your armor is sloppy—look, you are unfastened everywhere! Third, you say, "Speak to me, Lord, in Scripture; give me specific verses so I know exactly what You are saying to me." How can I bring you to My Word if you are lacking in it? You stare blankly at the Book, defenseless and unable to help yourself.

Are you who you say you are? You must

realize, dear one, what you have announced in the heavenlies about yourself; you have stated your position in My army with your mouth. Now, if you do not act out *from that position,* the enemy will surely tear you down. Do you think that because you say you are a warrior, he will run from you?

I woke you tonight to see if you would come to attention. I am doing this to many because I am testing them. If they do not hear My voice in the middle of the night and answer the call to pray, they are of little value to Me.

Understand the times and stop worrying about what *you* have to do. You are wasting time. I have a plan, and I will lead you; all you need to do is to be sensitive to My voice. I will lead you and guide you as the battle progresses. I need only for you to be prepared and stay ready.

Read, warrior, read! Fill yourself with hope and stand in faith. Especially tune your ear to the prophets of old; I am *still* speaking through them! Listen as I direct you by the wielding of the Word, and I will unveil My plan to you. Many will read the same words but will have no understanding. I have made it that way because I am calling the *true* warriors. Train them in your church, My people, My own—you are My own! You asked Me why I woke you, and I have spoken.

I held my Bible, asking, "Holy Spirit, where do I start?" I opened the Book, and my eyes focused solely on Isaiah 52:

Awake, awake; put on thy strength, O Zion; put on thy beautiful garments, O Jerusalem, the holy city. . . . Shake thyself from the dust; arise. . . . Therefore My people shall know My name: therefore they shall know in that day that I am He that doth speak: behold it is I (vv.1-2,6).

It is now 3:45 A.M. I have tarried for one hour; and yes, Lord, You have shown me things in Your Word, and You have talked to Me.

5
VOICE OF INSTRUCTION AND WARNING

Launch Out

Preach the Gospel. . . . Preach the Gospel. I want you to preach the Gospel. Learn it and preach it to all you know; preach it to all you don't know, for I am with you always, and I will help you. For I will be your guiding light that will shine forth to all you will meet. Please do My work on earth, as you are all I have to put forth My Father's word. Don't you see that *you* are all I have?

Blessed children of My Father, come forth and open your mouths. Tell everyone the truth so they may have eternal life with Me in heaven! Many will snicker and say, "Go away, you are insane; why don't you talk about what is real?" You are to say to them, "The truth is real. The truth is not an object that you can see, *yet you believe in the truth*. Why then is it so difficult to believe in God's Son, who is also truth? For He walked on this very earth!"

Do you see how simple-minded they will be? You must tell them simple things, for they do not know Me yet as you do. Be patient and gentle, because I am patient and gentle.I am in you, and you will work through Me and the Holy Spirit, who is all around you. Through Me, by the Holy Spirit, you will do My Father's work on earth.

You ask about your rewards? Oh yes, your rewards will be great and many, for you will have a high place near My Father—you will be glorified and exalted by angels. You will be loved beyond anything that you can imagine. You will feel great joy and happiness in that house. Oh, if I could tell you now; but I cannot, because for now you must live by faith. That is the way My Father chose it to be.

Now, you child, have a journey before you that will take you where you do not know; but I will be forever with you. Through you, I will smite the devil with the sword of My Word! You are a blessing in My eyes, and I burn with love for you with a fire that gives only heat, but cannot destroy. And *this* fire is My eternal love.

Blessed are all the children who come unto Me.

Come to Me

I pay attention to you. I am not like your friends who hear you, but are distracted by their own thoughts. There is no distraction in Me. I am not held back by time, nor am I persuaded by any other. When I set My eye on you, nothing will distract Me from communicating with you. I want to know your thoughts, and I want to receive your emotions. Do you understand how I am? There is none like Me who will commune with you.

I study your heart as you speak to Me, and I command My angels to give ear to your request. With whom, other than Me, will you spend your time? What is it that captures you, taking you away from me? Who do you desire, and at what table shall you dine? I beckon you intensely by My Spirit to come and have fellowship with Me, but you are too busy; you are preoccupied. How much of the time that I have given to you, will you spend with me?

These words are not to hurl insult at you, but to draw you to that which is the essence of your life. At times, you are carefree in My Spirit when you should be cautious. I want you to be inwardly still more often; otherwise, you could move about in a spirit that is not of Me.

You are so unaware, My child, of the danger

you invite when you do not stay close to Me. Be careful when you say, "In the spirit . . . in the spirit," and then run with the world. Be careful, I tell you, for there is one who *also* hungers after you! Do not grieve Me by ignoring My call to you, and do not vex Me by putting Me last every day. I am so patient and so willing to allow you to stretch in every direction, and I am so slow to anger. I cannot make you come to Me: I can only draw you.

You need to make a decision about whom and on what you will spend the time I have given you. You choose. If you want Me, you must come to the place where I am; *then* I will share with you the kingdom of heaven, and *then* I will reveal Myself to you—and *then* you will know Me. Ponder this!

The Supply Before You

My people say, "Give me Your heart, Oh Lord, so I might place it upon my own heart and feel what you feel toward your people."

But I say that when you received My robe of righteousness, you also received My heart. For you have been told to put on your robe of righteousness and to go forth in the spirit of grace that has been so lavishly poured out for you.

My people continually ask to be given more,

but they do not first eat what is already on their plate. They say, "More . . . more, Lord," before savoring and tasting, and putting into use that which they already abundantly have, even in their hands. Sometimes My people need to go back to their roots to be able to see all the rich morsels they now have set before them. How I long for a people of integrity in the things of the Spirit, and in opposition to the ways of the world and My enemy.

To quiet your tongue is what I desire, so that you are able to listen. Then, all of what you have already been given will be of good use for the glory and advancement of the kingdom of God.

Ask for My heart, Church, and keep on asking, because that is the very thing, above all others, that I wish for you to have; but know in your own heart what has already been supplied to you. You need to draw from the plate before you, not letting any of what I have put there be distasteful in your sight. I have given you a balance, and you need to consume each thing I have put before you.

Then the robe of righteousness, My heart, My compassion, and My will shall surround you in all that you put your hands to. Let the robe cover you; and in so doing, you will walk under the presence of God. You must know the *value* of this robe, for it is My covering over you.

Under it, you will love as I do, see as I do, be diligent as I am, and you will have great peace.

Seek wisdom so that you will gain understanding. Be steadfast so that you will not miss the sound of My voice. Be courageous, knowing that I, the Lord, am your strength, sheltering you from *every* storm and bringing you into everlasting life—a life of joy, a life of laughter, a life without burdens, and a life of perfected integrity. For now you are to strive in the Spirit as one who runs. For if you do not strive *in the Spirit,* you will stumble and grow weary, lacking in the very thing you asked for—My heart.

Beware of Self

When you boast of yourself,
    it is not from Me.
If you continue to boast in yourself,
    you will not have Me.

Blessed are those who hold their tongue
    and let others speak.
Blessed are those who have concern
    for their fellow man.
He who thinks he knows all, cannot hear
    anything.
But he who is hungry will learn much.

I tell you, be careful with that tongue,
  for you do not know its power.

Stay in My Word.
I tell you this for your righteousness.
Continue to walk in My way and be humble.
For My Father will not know those who are
  proud in themselves.

———— ••• ————

Instruction

Love and guidance,
  not interference and haste.
Hold your tongue when it is not
  for you to decide and lend guidance
  instead.
You are not to show the way,
  but to follow the way.
Let others live their lives—
  and you are to live yours.
Always show love and compassion to all.
And through your love,
  they will see Me.

———— ••• ————

Beware of Man's Glory

The sons of man shall blow their horns and
say triumphant words. Woe to them who set
themselves up as most high in this world. I tell

you the truth, if any man exalts himself before men, he will not be exalted before Me. Men have such foolishness in their hearts, and their tongues are drunk; what they have to say is of no importance. Woe unto them that shun the light! But My words bring life.

If someone knew that today would be his last, would he still laugh with drunken merriment? Would he rejoice in what he has made of himself? Would he speak of his accomplishments? No! If he knew that this was his last day, he would cry out to Me and say, "Lord, help me!" He would cry, "Why me—what have I ever done?" But I would say to him when he is finished, *you* never knew Me. While you were busy gathering up the social graces of this world, you missed the grace of your Father in heaven. But weren't you laughing just a moment ago? Wasn't your world complete? Then why now do you cry out to Me? Man is so foolish to gamble with time. Doesn't he know that he gambles with what is not his, but Mine? The things I have given man for free can never be purchased, nor can they be had by begging, only by living.

So when the drunk says, "Please, Lord," to whom is he speaking? Who listens? Does he cry with repentance in his heart? He says, "Repentance . . . what is that?"

That none should perish—that they would

know and accept the love of My Father—is the desire of Jesus Christ. I tell you that the Spirit of the Living God beckons them to receive, but they do not hear. How sad it is for some men of this world, never to have known their Father.

———◆◆◆———

Idols

You shall have no other gods before you. They are My enemy; rebuke them in the name of Jesus. Your eyes see what many eyes do not see. Let them test the spirit; what *I* have given you cannot be rebuked or sent away. *I* put My image in your heart and your spirit, so that no one could be mistaken that it is I who dwells within you!

Mercy. Mercy to those who seek the truth. Know My Word, and know that it is true. Do not put any graven images before Me. Do not set your eyes on anything but My Spirit. Do not fall in love with what your eyes see. Do not become captivated. Do not be consumed with anything that man has made.

———◆◆◆———

What Is My Concern?

My concern is first with You, God, my Father, in whom all things are created. My concern is my relationship with You before anything else: before my worries, before my cares, before anything. Lord have mercy—if I could only get that straight!

And He says:

Receive of Me, and the doors of heaven will be opened to you. Why do you persist so in carrying your burdens and troubles? Look, I stand before you. Won't you hand them to Me? Now pray first for yourself, the needs of your family, and those who are close to you; that way there will be sufficient time to pray for others. There is power in order, and I am orderly.

Don't search the skies for names of those who need prayer, but make yourself whole—that way you are equipped for the concern of others. Yes, bind up the evil one; he cannot raise havoc when you are in My will. Stand firm in what I have given you, and do not fall prey to the enemy's lies.

When you are with Me on that glorious day, it will be because of the choices you have made. To be a part of My kingdom, you had to choose Jesus; but it was your choice. You are continually given instruction, both from My Word and from My voice, but again it is your choice to live in my way.

Be Still

But now I say to you, ask for nothing and seek nothing; otherwise, you are only seeking what *you* want. Be still so that I might fill you with My desire. Do not search the heart of God with your mind, but rest intently in the Spirit. When you are anxious, the time you have allowed for Me is quickly consumed, and you will leave empty.

Learn to wait on Me in anticipation that you *will* receive. The things I have for you are gifts that cannot be achieved through your works. So do not fret My child, but rest in peace in Me.

———◆——◆——◆———

Walk on the Word

And the Spirit of the Lord says:

Stand on the Word. Walk on it. Let it move with you under your feet. Keep it strapped to the soles of your feet. Never lift a foot unless it is attached. Don't be afraid to lose it when you move. Keep in mind that it is always there. Become rooted in it. Stay by the Word and don't wander, least you be devoured.

Do not defile the grace on which you stand; become united in grace for which you stand. Having done all this, know for sure that you cannot be shaken.

Now your feet are not heavy—they are lifted on the wings of the Lord. Now stop directing the way in which they will go, for you do not know the way, and you will get lost. Let go of what you know in your head, and let the feet of the Righteous One direct your path. As you become secure in your steps, you will know how to love.

Blessed are the hungry, for they *will* be fed.

Give me understanding, and I will keep your law and obey it with all my heart. Direct me in the path of Your commands, for there I find delight (Psalms 119:34).

A Message

Lord, look at us down here, so lost and small, gathering all our worldly goods . . . gathering . . . gathering.

And He says:

What good will all you have gathered do you in the end? Will it protect you, save you, or bring you peace? How you hide from Me behind your possessions. Why do you hide from Me? I love you. Come away from what you do not need and follow Me. I will give you glorious things that you have never known. I will show you spectacular things far beyond where you are! That which you now own will be of little value. But that which you can seek will be worth more than all man's gold.

I am telling you a most beautiful thing: To possess what I am is a gift of eternity. Look for Me, search and find Me. Your blessings will be great.

What Is Your Opinion?

First, your opinion is exactly that—*your* opinion—which means not the will of God. If one is truly a servant of the Most High God, then what place is there for your opinion? Your opinion is what *you* think—*not* what Christ revealed and *not* Him being glorified. Greater than this is the difference in opinions. Now, God's wisdom has been *completely* put aside; and in *its* place, mere human thought resides.

So the real question is, "What is human thought?" The enemy is very sly, you know; and he will not be defeated by your opinion. Do you understand? What have your thoughts to do with God's work? What have they to do among the brothers? I tell you that your opinion can do nothing except separate the love that I desire you to have for one another. Who are you to exalt yourself against the knowledge of Christ?

Now . . . what is your opinion?

The Window in Your Heart

If you are like-minded with Me, why do you not see your brother as I see him? Why do you not love him as I love him? Look in the churches; do you not see the cold hearts? So many say they are hungering for Me, but they do not truly love their brother. How much more are you able to give from your heart than you do? When will you see each other as I see you? Yes, you *can* see this way because you have been given the mind of Christ. If you truly want to know Me better, you will love your brother as I love you. Think about why I chose you: Was it not that you would also choose Me?

It is in My consideration of the condition in the hearts of My beloved that causes Me great concern. My Church remains entangled in the ways of the world, having more concern for the preoccupations of this world than the need for one another. The worldliness in the Church makes My people blind, just as an angel of light, Satan, has blinded them. Lift the scales from your eyes and come to the understanding of Whom you are from and why you exist!

While My Spirit cries out for holiness within you, you also cry out for holiness from within. What brings holiness? Have you love in your heart? From whom? What and whom do you love? Are you more concerned with a lifestyle than you are concerned for the pain in your brother's heart? Look around at one another; what do you see? Did I not send you to bind up the brokenhearted? Are you doing so? My love is intensified within the Body when the brothers truly love the brothers.

If you want more of Me, as you say you do, you too must be willing to lay down your life, not so much in the physical, but in your mind's focus on the world. If you will take your eyes off the things of the world, the scales will fall from your eyes.

My Church, My beautiful Church, when will you see each other as I see you? When will you see each other with the eyes of your heart? There is a window there; look out from the window of your heart! How I love you, My Church.

Curiosity

Do not be curious. Do not have curiosity; instead, seek only wisdom! The things of the world will draw you by your senses, but the Word of God confirms reality. Be curious for nothing; be steadfast in everything, having gained the knowledge of Christ. Do not therefore become tempted by the words and ways of the world. The world hates My presence in you! Wake up, My child, and realize to Whom you belong.

What does a drifter and a man who is settled in his home have in common? Nothing! Neither do you have things in common with those who do not proclaim My name. My name is Jesus! While you are wondering about some of the things of the world, are you shouting that name? You have been called *peculiar* because I have deliberately fashioned you to be that way, so that the world could tell you *apart*—apart from them. Stop looking around! What do you expect to find? For what are you searching, and what is your goal? To whom do you belong—and are you faithful to that one?

I see your ways. Nothing is hidden from Me; I know the very intentions of your heart. Choose which way you will go: either a way filled with curiosity for the unknown, or a committed way of life under the rule of My Word. You cannot live half in the world and half in the knowledge of Christ. So, what will you do?

Take time to consider your ways. Take a long look at all of what you are. Look very deeply into your own soul. What is it that hurts you, and why are you afraid? Are you your own god? Who are you? What do you want? How much is your life worth? At what cost can you be purchased? Don't you see, My child? Don't you understand? Without Me, you are like a newborn pup rejected by its mother, hopeless and with no future—the future of which I speak is eternal life.

This life is only but a breath—you know this is true. Don't you see that at the very moment when everyone rejects you, My arms are opened wide for you to come to Me? Such a struggle all the time for you, child of curiosity, and such disappointments. I will allow you time now to decide what you will do. Remember that you cannot choose the middle; it must be one or the other. I have created you for Myself, to love you and to have fellowship with you; but the only way I will come to you is if you invite Me in. This is the way I have created it to be, My child.

------◆◆◆------

What About Different Churches?

Don't worry about others—I will take care of them. You know now when things are from Me and when things are not. You are to go with what is in your heart, where all things are done for Me and in worship of Me. There can be no wrong when they are from Me. You know what I have taught you; see what you know from Me, for Me?

And don't worry about what anyone else does. You take care of yourself, and I will have charge of the world. Let them worship as they wish—they cause Me no harm. Stay in grace as I have shown you. Listen only to Me, for I am your counselor. Let no one but Me guide you at all times.

You are good because you listen to your Father and do as I ask. You know in your heart now what many do not know. Use that knowledge to praise and worship Me, for it is for your salvation. I know you understand.

Go on with life as you know it, and do good things, as I know you will. Remember to be kind and caring when people treat you with indifference, because that will happen.

Do not follow anyone but Me. Do not listen to anyone but Me. Do not worship anyone but Me.

Your heart tells you the truth; search for it continually, and do not be deceived, My child.

———— ◆ ◆ ————

Pollution

Lord, why do I feel so angry, like I want to throw this thing that angers me off a cliff?

He says:

It is because the ways of the world are being poured into you and unto your spirit. You have opened yourself to the workings of men's minds, and they have stuffed their knowledge into you. Your body breathes in and out; and wherever you choose to be, you will breathe in that very thing. You are an open vessel; I made you that way. If you walk with people who speak mixed words and you try to mingle with them, you will absorb what they say. That is why, after you received Me, you had need to stay in Me and full of Me.

Remember that you will receive the desire of your heart. When you give ear to the enemy, he *will* fill it. Now you want to get rid of it, because the taste of it is affecting you spiritually. It is not difficult: Renounce it, rout it out, turn it over, and be set free. In the name of Jesus—it is that name that sets you free! (see Philippians 2:10)

Warning in Relationships

Do not be deceived, little one. The enemy lies in wait for you, like a lion in the bushes. Stay behind Me, says the Spirit of the Lord, and do not try to get ahead of Me. There is danger all around; but it need not come near your tent as long as I am your covering.

Do not be hasty when you speak—you have been told this before. Wait and be steadfast; otherwise, your own words will sweep you away from Me right into the enemy's snare. Do not be deceived with soft-spoken words. Do you think the enemy spoke with a shout or with a whisper to Eve? You need to draw closer to Me. You are just a child, and your plan will bring disaster to you.

Be still and listen, and do not be concerned with what others think when you don't socially mingle as they think you should. They are My concern, and you are My concern; but you are not each other's concern! That is why I say to speak to each other through Scripture. In that way, you will stay in obedience to Me, and you will not become ensnared.

Are you beginning to understand? Do you hear the wisdom of My words? Do they satisfy? You are to seek to know Me and My ways, not those of the world. I am not of the world and neither are you; so why do you partake in the ways of it? I have put a *"red flag of danger"* within you. If you will be sensitive to the Spirit, you will plainly see it; when you do, stop whatever you are doing or saying, and come aside—then I, who loves you, will give you guidance. You do not need to give the world an answer for every decision you make, so stop feeling obligated to join in conversation.

Be careful, little one. For just as I love you intently, so does the evil one hate you! It is right to have fellowship with one another, but if you allow Me to choose your friends, you will remain safe behind My covering. Choose your own way and be exposed; or listen to My choice and be protected. They will hate you because of Me, *because they cannot control you*—this is the whole reason.

Divided in Self

What have you in your heart, and what is your heart's desire? Anger, strife, frustration—are these the issues of your heart? Judgment—is there judgment in your heart? (Matthew 12:34) Hurt, pride, self-pity?

You say, "God, I pray your will be done in this situation." Your words and your heart are not in agreement. You seek Me with your words, but your heart is what I hear. Your heart is very clear to My eyes and My ears; but your words are contrary, and they lie about your true condition. Are you beginning to understand? No, your heart is not broken, for only I can break it—it is merely wounded.

You say your spirit is also wounded. Is your pain too great? Nevertheless, I am here, and I will bring you through. Do not judge anyone, for in the same way, you will be judged. If your heart and your words cannot line up, how much less are you able to judge the issues of God? I am bringing correction to you so you may have life more abundantly! Isn't that what you want?

Then you are to stand firm in truth and allow Me to do the rest. Stop trying to assist Me. For you cannot at any time assist Me, because you do not know My ways; there will come a time when you will, but now you do not. It is important that you be still so that I might bring about a good work in you. So much of what you say is meaningless, and you tire yourself in it.

Come away into My riches—the Word I gave you—that you may dance, play and sing in the anointing. Walk away from the world, and come with Me. Come and have peace, rest and joy. Come.

Frustration

Frustration leads to death! "Why," you say? What use has yarn when it is full of knots and tangles? Come, let us reason. Look at yourself and examine what is within. What causes you to be this way? Was it the circumstance, or was it already there, waiting to be triggered? Who has done this to you?

You are still full of insecurity, and you still rely on man to comfort you. A seed of bitterness was sown into you when you were young, and it has grown into a tree. It matters not who did it. What matters is the choice you now make to keep it or to cut it down. Think carefully, because this decision *will change your entire life.* You have been fighting against it, trying to be free from it, but it always returns when you are provoked. Anger is not the enemy; it is *frustration,* the inability to function under stress.

Are you beginning to understand? Shall we cut the whole tree down just because all of the branches are bad? Yes, most assuredly so. For what use will the tree itself have aside from its branches? Let us begin to cut down the tree, and then make sure that all the roots are removed so that none of them will send up a new shoot; for you may be unaware for a time should this happen.

Say now, "In the name of Jesus, I apply His blood to my bitter fruit, and I cut back the branches, so that I might see and take down the whole tree."

Which Way?

Where is the right church, Lord? Give me direction, for many hold so many different ceremonies to reach and worship You.

And He says:

For the wrath of My Father is fire and fury. The Commandments were written so all would know the way. Many miracles were shown so everyone would know the way. I walked and died and rose, so all would know the way. I gave My Word so everyone would know.

What is it that you need? Do you think you need the word of man, when you already have the Word of God? I know this was asked for another and not for yourself; I know you asked this for a loved one, because I am in you, and where I rest, some questions have no value. But now you have the answer for those who ask. Tell them to open their ears and listen to the sound of the Lord. As they hear the Word, they *will* receive!

. . . and where the Spirit of the Lord is, there is liberty (2 Corinthians 3:17).

What J Have

O Lord, You are so good; my heart is overflowing. What do I do to deserve such gifts from You?

And He says:

You believe. See what comes when you believe! Be happy, always trust, never doubt! Keep My commands and you will never be without. I take care of those who are in Me and of Me. I, the Lord, will keep you. Count your blessings—you cannot, for they are too many. As always, give praise and glory to God.

6

RUNNING FROM GOD

How Long Will You Sleep?

Oh, My child, how long will you sleep? It is morning, and I speak to you; but you will not listen. Who has blocked your ears? Who has blinded you? I look at you, and I weep because you ignore the love I have for you. You say you are unworthy; but I say you are among the righteous! I do not see you as you see yourself—I see you perfected!

How long will you reject the One who gave His life for you? How long will you turn your back on the One who saves? Do you not know that Jesus shed His blood for your sins *already*? What is wrong? What more can I do? The price has already been paid! If you do not listen, you will surely die. I cannot go against what has been written; I cannot lie. So now I come to you this way in writing, to appeal to that which I have put in you even before you were born—in your spirit. If you had but one day left, would you still deny Me?

If You Don't Know Me

You can call it what you want—you're still in Satan's realm. For you and all who are like you, He gave His Life. When the Father said, "Do you love the child so much that you would die for his transgressions?"

Jesus' answer was, "Yes."

Do you not now understand what love is? Do you not know that the Son gave the ultimate gift of Himself to you and for you? Do you not know that His Spirit was sent back to you so that you may still know Jesus Christ intimately, just as if He were still here walking with you? Let there be no doubt as to what He did for you. Why then do you doubt? Read what I have left for you so that you may know all truth.

Abide in My ways, and I will show you a kingdom of glory in this world *and* in that which is to come.

Come follow Me.

———◆◆———

The Hardened Heart

There is power in the Word.
There is great power in the Word.
Like a never-ending wheel that rolls around
    the hardened hearts of men.

And the wheel of the Word starts to chip,
and it rolls along the outside of that heart—
and it chips and chips and chips.

And then the curtain of darkness begins to fall,
    because its boundaries are weakened.
Then the Light begins to penetrate,
    through the gaps caused by the wheel.

And the heart starts to listen to the beautiful
    music of the Word it could never hear
    before—
And the heart begins to grow hungry,
    and slowly starts to reach out to be fed.

Praise and glory to You, O Lord,
    for Your patience among men.
There are no words to express Your patience.

His Nearness

Child of the Lord, how beautiful you are.
When you cry out, I hear you every time. I am
saddened that you cannot yet see. Your burdens
are heavy because you carry them alone. Oh, My
sweet child, give them to Me and I will carry
them away from you to a place far beyond, and
they will find you no longer. Peace and happiness

are yours for the asking. These things are free—
like a gift. Just think of Me and ask! You are My
child, and I want you with Me. Do you understand? Within you lies a place where you may
have My rest. When I rest with you, I bring all
good things—many that you know, and many
that you cannot yet know. But you will know all
in time to come.

Precious one, do not be afraid. I cannot
bring you harm, but only good things. I am the
One who knows how many hairs you have on
your head. And no harm will come to even one
of them: I know—they were made by Me. Many
great promises have been made—some to na-
tions and some to people like you—and they all
will be kept. It is all the same to Me, for you are
as important as a nation to Me. When you feel
that pang in your heart, it is I, asking that you
let Me in. Your heart is the place where I come
and stay.

I ask you to consider what I have said to you.
Consider it in your heart first rather than your
mind, because your mind can tell you untrue
things; but your heart has the truth. I am not
speaking of emotions at all, but your heart; you
know what I am saying.

Do not let the darkness of this world over-
shadow your life. You have the power to be free
from it. Take up your armor with Me, and war
against everything of this world that holds you

down. Fight, but fight in My way with Me; I will stand beside you. I will hold you up; you will not fall.

Let Me bring a smile to your lips and put happiness in your heart. Listen to the music I have for you. It is so beautiful.

You see, I am of pure love, and all that I do is for love of you. Don't you see? Look and keep looking: I am so close you can touch Me. I am your Father . . . your Father that made you!

Do not be alarmed because of these words. I use those who love and obey Me; the one who is writing is a vessel for Me, so that the words I speak might be received by you. This writing is for My glory only. As each of My children come to Me, they are tested; they are given tasks to do of Me. They do them gladly, with joy, and without question. This writing was given to you from My power, through the one who writes it. The one writing understands little of what is said because it is meant for you, the reader.

Be with people who know Me; they are your brothers and sisters in faith. They will guide you and help you. Remember all that I promise you is forever. Not one thing will ever be taken away from you. You will find love like you have never known *in* Me. You will have joy and harmony in your house, which is your body. Oh, little one so precious to Me, come.

The Undecided Heart

The soul says that while we are in this world, casting stones has a part in all we do. Gossip seems a necessary tool of life. While casting aspersions upon others, we are in hopes of raising ourselves higher in the eyes of those we admire. It is not that we wish them harm; we do not. We do it so others will sense our knowledge and find us interesting and intelligent. How are we to know the damage we cause?

And He says:

Cast not aspersions on those you love.

Cast not aspersions on those you hate.

Cast not aspersions on those you do not know.

But listen to your heart, My child, for there lies the truth. The truth about everything. There lies wisdom of all good things of the world and of that which is to come.

You see, My child, you are so important to me that I would allow you to live your life as you choose. And there is not one set way that you must be. But as you listen to your Father who is in your heart, peace and harmony will come upon you. For when you have Me, you have everything!

And when you have everything, you have no need for those of the world to grant you acceptance. When you have Me, the wisdom you will gain will far exceed man's knowledge. You will not need man to give you direction; I will do that.

There are many more things to tell you, dear child, but they will be held for another time. Have faith in that which you do not know. All things will be made clear to you when you believe. Let your heart be light, and let My love flow through. The beauty of My love will far surpass any that you have ever known. May My words stay in your heart. May your words reflect the truth. Always remember that *I* am the truth. I will be ever faithful to you. Look for Me; I am here.

———————◆◆———————

A Heartfelt Cry From One Lost Sheep

Oh Father, I am so small inside. I'm not allowed to speak; I am so oppressed. I am so lonely. I ache for You, but I am trapped within this dirty body. I have soiled what You gave me; I have dirtied myself. I have ruined my white gown. Father, look at me and see me as I am. I am not worthy to come before you, nor can I. I hurt so much. I cry inside all the time. I am being tormented by evil, even now, as I speak to You. Everything inside me feels like it is ripping apart; my heart aches. Where is my heart? I don't know. Oh, what am I? I am wretched and miserable. I detest what I have become. I played the enemy's game, and he has consumed me. I fear for my life. I don't want to die, but I am close to death.

Lord, I have no hunger for You; I wish to be hungry, but yet I cannot eat. I think I will starve and that the evil one will have me in death. Oh, Jesus, where are you? My heart cries out to you. Do you not hear me? Why? Why?—Oh, the pain....

Please, please, I beg You to help me. Why don't You help me? You helped them, but You won't help me. Why? What have I done that You won't even talk to me? I can't help it now, don't You see? Blackness is all around me. I read Your Word, I try to pray, but You won't even look at my face. Am I so ugly? Am I so grotesque? Am I so unwanted? I cry, and I cry, and I cry.

But He says :

My child, yes, you are wretched, and your ways are evil. But look, I will show you a way out. Take the child within you (your spirit) and run; run away from the evil one who holds you captive in chains. You can do this if only you will take My hands. You are in a pit of thick mud, but I can set you free.

ᵧy is in you. My peace abounds. My rock
ι. Come forth into the hands of righteousness. For the wretched shall become righteous—even you, O wretched one. I will not
leave you or forsake you, for I am your Father
who made you. I will not allow the evil one to
destroy what I have made in beauty. I will save
you from his clutches, and I will take you away
with Me. I will pull you into My arms. I will encompass you with a love that you have never
known. I will be your Comforter. I will be your
strength and your glory.

I have a place for you, My child—a beautiful
place. You will come and play in My house, and I
will give you a place to rest your head. You are so
weary and tired—come, let Me give you rest.
Come.

Turn Around

What do you fear? What is it that tortures
you on your insides? Who is it that loves a lie?
Who is it who comes to steal, kill and destroy
YOU? Is it God, the Lord Jesus, who stands before you in love, and who pours out His Holy
Spirit on you? Whom do you love? Whom do
you choose? Which one will hold out a gold coin
to you, but when you reach out to take it, it
changes to rubbish?

What do you want, child? Say it out loud with your mouth. Your journey is very short in this life, or don't you know this fact already? What can you accomplish? What can you do, anyway? What have you ever done to change anything? Nothing, you say, and that is correct—nothing!

When will you stop? Or will you? You decide for yourself how you will be and what you will become. Surely you cannot fool yourself . . . can you? And if you could, for what purpose?

The same promise has been made to you as it has for all men—the promise of life everlasting. It is already awarded to you, but only *if* you repent of your own evil ways, turn your life around, and no longer associate yourself with those who hate God.

Jesus paid the price; you know that! So do what you will, because the one thing God has given you, your own free will, will never be taken away. **All those in hell still cry to change what they have chosen, but the ears of the Lord listen only to those who are still alive.**

Why Do You Hesitate?

Hold onto the Word with all your might, as if it were a rope, a lifeline to you. Hold on with both hands, and do not let it go. There is no other way in which you can serve God—there is no other way. If you hold on with only one hand, you will still slip and fall.

You say you are frightened; why then do you stand out in the cold when the door is open before you? Why don't you come in? Others come in and stay warm, but you continue to stand outside and shake. It is your decision; nevertheless, I wait for you. Holy and righteous is My name! Why do you hesitate, when the cost of your freedom has already been paid? In Christ, I gave My best for you, because I have loved you from the beginning.

Open Your Heart

O Lord, how much longer will You endure the rejection of man?

And He says:

From the beginning there were great signs, and through all time, there were more; but some stood with straight faces. When God's fury has come, they will be straight no more.

It is for you to understand My mercy, My patience, and My love for you. Everything is for you; open your hearts and accept what I give you freely. Accept what I give you now, and soon everything will be yours.

Do you understand? You will receive great

gifts that will bring you even more gifts. Open your heart and take them: they are yours for the asking. Say, "Yes," to Me. Don't delay; the time is near. But if I am with you, you will know no fear.

Hear these words, and turn around.

7

WORDS OF WISDOM

Time

Can you understand waiting? Can you accept patience? Are you aware of time and what it is—and the purpose of it? What do you know of the expanse? What is vastness?

Do not fret and become overburdened with these things, as none of them are of concern to you. They are only highways of travel for you. Do not be alarmed when time itself seems to be passing by and you have not yet completed what you set out to do in that portion of time. Be diligent in your obedience to Me, but do not concern yourself with what you cannot control.

There is much to be completed in time as you know it, and it will all be done. The things that I have predestined to be, will be for your good. In this very moment, what are you able to do? Can you wait for this moment? Can you wait for several? You should understand by now that those who have put their trust in Me also travel with Me in My time—no longer where they were.

Because of salvation, there has also been a transition. I will reveal to you a mystery: If you will set yourself solely on the Son of God and seek Him with all your heart, you will find yourself removed from time; you will find yourself in the expanse.

So do not become troubled when all that you have set out to do seems unfinished, for I collect your very thoughts, not only your deeds, and I examine the intentions of the heart. Be still as you labor. Do not be restless. Seek the things that preserve inward peace and go about your day doing good for the Lord your God. Hold fast to your vision, because I shall bring it about; but you need only go day by day. You need not be concerned with anything beyond that; otherwise you will waste the very thing I supply you with each new day. Rest within and know that I am He who masters the universe. Surely I will not forget what I have called you to, and surely I will see you through.

Come and Grow

What is it you ask? If I tell you the answer, will you obey? I tell you that these times of strife will come again and again, but the confusion of the world is not yours to bear.

Father, is it true that the more that you give me of Yourself, the harder my life will be—that it will be more for me to remember and more difficult to stay on Your path?

And He replies:

Oh no, child of Mine—not more difficult, but more glorious. You make Me smile when you ask those questions; you're still so fearful. Remember, I will never leave you nor forsake you. I do not intend to allow you to live on your own, but under the constant protection of My shadow. As you continue to give more of yourself, you are not losing, but gaining.

You don't always understand what is happening to you—that is why you must absolutely trust in Me. I know; whereas you do not know. I am the source of all power. I am all that I am, and I am all! How can you not rely on Me? I cannot go away from you. I made you to be with Me and cannot change My Word to you. I do not want you to fear My presence within you, but I do want you to thirst for more of Me. Be hungry, and I will feed you.

You are still a wanderer, even though you

think you are stable. Apart from Me, you can do nothing. Fear not, for I am with you. I am the Lord your God, and I care for you; I will never leave you: For you are in need of Me at all times. When you are glad, you share with Me your happiness; and when you are sad, you also share with Me. We are becoming closer, and I do not want you to fear this closeness. I want you to seek even more; and when you do have more, continue to seek more. Do not ever stop, for I am your heart's desire, and I long for you—I love you so.

So, My child, do not hold Me at bay; welcome Me into your house, for one day you will come into My house. Uphold My laws, for they are holy and just. See to it that you set yourself as an example of My Son. Live your life in purity and in simpleness, not striving for the things of man, but for the Spirit; that is where your treasure lies.

Breath Me in. Ask Me to fill you. Receive My wisdom, which you so greatly desire. I am your Father, and I care for you.

Blessed be My children, for My children bless Me.

. . . Apart from Me, you can do nothing (John 15:5).

Conscience

Conscience? It is not yours as you think, but mine. It is the sound of My voice within you. No, it is not in your head, but it is all through you. This I say to you, yours is not to *know My way*, but you are to *know of My ways*. Do you see? I speak to you, but you do not hear Me until I have spoken; therefore, you cannot know before I tell you.

Precious are you who ask questions of your Father pertaining to your very self. When you have knowledge and wisdom, you have strength in the Lord your God. Those who do not listen to their conscience have hearts that are hard. I am still there as I am in everyone; but when one ignores Me, I do not speak. How sad it is for some to not know love, for I am love and the extension of the Father who is within you.

So that voice you hear is the glorious sound of the Lord your God. Never turn it away, but listen intently to it always in everything you do. Accept what I tell you, for it is true; no man should doubt.

Reliance

Go to the top of the mountain, for there in the valley below lies the answer. You must be able to lift yourself above your burdens to be able to see them clearly. When you can see them clearly, then you can come out from under them. Face not the depths of hell, but face the kingdom of heaven, for this is where all truth lies.

My child, why are you so concerned? Will your being concerned change one day of your life? Let it go and give it to Me. I hold the key to all knowledge and direction. If you will keep behind Me, I will show you those things that you do not yet know. You keep asking and asking, but do you ever *rely*? I have not seen that. You say you *trust* in Me, but you have not yet *relied* on Me; this is why you are having problems. Don't be discouraged, for this is a most difficult thing to do. Many seek Me, but few attain the fullness of My Spirit.

You must learn to relax in Me so that I may work in you. Don't fall asleep, but be alert in My Word. I will help you to find Scripture to support your every need, now that you have truly learned to ask. Drink in the wisdom of the Lord, for it has been put before you, and for all to see.

Go to the mountain with Me, and I will show you your house.

Morsels Along the Path

Because of Me, the world calls you a fanatic. Ask yourself, "*Who* has peace—them or you?"

Because you love Me, they will hate you. They hate you only because they do not understand.

When you are slow to speak and eager to listen, you quiet the mouth of the lion.

Patience is better than money. If you have the first, it is enough. If you have the second, it is *never* enough.

Encourage your enemy; in that way, he will see his wrongdoing. Go up against him, however, and he will hate you all the more.

Consider the grass; consider the animals. Now consider man. Which of these have been given My grace? That one has My inheritance.

How long is time? Who can measure it? What is the distance from home? Can you be there when you are away?

You can climb the mountains in the sea; when you reach the top, you will still be under. So it is with the world.

Quiet is the nature of a wise man, and obstinacy is the way of rebellion.

How wide is the sky when you are looking from beneath it!

Help a friend, help a stranger; in so doing, you are the one receiving help.

With all the money and riches of the *world*, a king is only as great as his servant.

Jezebel ruled with the power of persuasion, but meekness moves with the power of grace.

The greatest attribute of fear is its ability to grip!

Fear is never faithful; only a fool has trust in it. But to fear God is to behold Him.

How long, O world, will you look only at the surface, never deeper than your own face in the mirror?

You who check the distance of the stars, how far is heaven—can you plot the course?

If a man is to live on earth more than once, what is the purpose of the first life? What from the first will the second avail?

Why sit in sorrow, when each moment that passes is dead—a collection of emptiness.

Sorrow will not bring comfort, but a good laugh brings relief!

8

HE LOVES ME

From His Eyes

My dearest child,
of whom I'm so proud,
In heaven they know you;
your voice rings out loud.
With trumpets accompanying
the words from your heart,
Angels rejoice because you do your part.

Such majesty reigns above and below.
Our Lord and our Savior,
His triumph will show.
To all those He's given
the joy of His love,
Much more will be added,
great gifts from above.

He says, "From the day you were born,
you were destined to be,
A brave, mighty warrior
dressed in splendor for Me."

Such Love

Forever true, as purple is to the grape;
forever true I am to you.
Everlasting, as time in eternity,
everlasting is My love toward you.
Deep emotion,
as the springs under the river,
deep emotions have I, longing for you!

As My eyes rest upon *all* of mankind,
Behold, I give all My time to *you*.
I'll never leave you; I'm always there.
Don't you wonder how this can be?
I bestow many gifts upon you.
I am like this to all those who worship Me,
for I hold all of love beyond measure.

Someday you will understand
why I am this way;
then you will come to know.
See, I have great compassion,
as the lion is tender with her cubs.
And see the beauty I hold before you,
like a lily—no, a rose!
I love you. I love you.
Receive in abundance from Me.

Love

What is love? Love is a lifetime decision. It is a decision to look at every circumstance with eyes of forgiveness. It is a decision to consider your brothers' needs a little more than your own. Love is an encourager, always shedding light on every dark moment. Love is also a mystery that the human mind cannot perceive nor understand.

Love is not an emotion, but presents itself as a person. Love is grace, and the *understanding* of grace. Love never tires. Love never faints. Love never disappoints. Love is assurance, and love is always capable. Love is never short on time. Love is not limited to time, nor does it count it. Love always desires to give and to serve.

Love is both silent and loud, and can be seen in everything; yet it is *never* possessive. Love waits and is not moved by the mind's mental condition. It surpasses all things that are natural to man, often leading him in a lifetime search of it. Love consumes hate and brings freedom to a harnessed soul. Love is beyond the world, yet exists in spite of it.

Love abounds only in truth. Any form of love without truth is not love; without love, there can be no truth. Love and truth are one. When all that we are will one day pass away, love remains forever. Love is eternal. A man who knows love will live forever in it. Love is the beginning and will be the end of all things, because love is complete. Now *this* is love.

Intense Love

He says:

"Magnify, magnify," you say to Me. What are you magnifying? Can You be magnified? Can I be made larger than I am? Do you know My size?

I want you to come into worship in total precision from within your spirit. Magnify My heartbeat within you; magnify the ability I have given to you to do so. Lift and pull on everything I have poured into you. Do not praise and sing from your mouth, but from your depths.

Magnify . . . magnify. Increase your instruments. Go from a violin to a complete orchestra, knowing that My presence is ushered in on the very sound of your voice. Even when you sing from within, with your mouth closed, it is as trumpets were going off in the heavenlies. That is why I say to praise Me continually, every moment, in everything you do.

Ah, for the glory of the glory! I have set myself in your midst—look, here I am! Has My glory filled your temple? Release all that you are, so that I may consume all that you are not. My love for you is intense, and my desire to fill you is ever present. I want to fill you; let My Spirit flow from the top of your head to the tip of your toes. You are My own; let Me love you.

I knew you before, and I have not forgotten you. You are my love forever. There is no one else like Me who can love you this way. In spite of how you see yourself, you are My treasure!

———— ◆◆ ————

Lost in the Beauty

Are you happy in prayer?

I answered, *"Yes."*

Are you at peace?

"Yes," I said.

Then write this:

"I sing praise to your name, Lord. For the Lord is love and worthy to be praised. I will lift up my hands in praise to You. Lift up my hands in praise to You, and Your light will shine upon my waiting heart.

"I will glorify Your name, My Lord. Glorify your name, Lord. For Your peace is here, and I will flow with You.

"You are beautiful to me, Lord—beautiful to me, Lord. For the stars that sparkle far beyond the sky are Yours, worthy just for You; for their light is great, and all power comes from You.

"With Your glorious magnitude, You rest

upon my heart like a dove. Oh, everlasting One, how wonderful You are!"

I Am Like the Sun

Like the sun's rays, which touch everything, so am I! One can feel their warmth, as if he were the only one to feel it. He can completely lose himself on a cold day in the warmth of the sun's rays. One in the North and one in the South can both at the same time feel the exact same warmth enveloping their bodies in peacefulness.

When you are cold, does the sun not warm you? Such am I among men. I am the same for all men. I can be felt by all, just as if each man were the only person on earth. Do you see how I am?

You can have Me in the depths of your heart, as if there were no one but the two of us; but I am like this to all—and all at the same time.

When you think of the sun's rays touching everything on the earth, think of Me.

I Heard Your Song

For the melody of a broken heart is sweet music to My ears. You are as a song of waters rolling against the stones. You are very wonderful to Me, and I listen intently as you send up praise to Me. For I am holy and deserving of all your praise.

Have I not given you a new song, and have I not also given you the melody and a voice to sing it? When you sing to Me, you are pouring out your love for Me in adoration of My name. Isn't it wonderful to be able to love?

Be still, child, for a little while, and let me minister to you. I want you to lie down in the shade of a tree and allow Me entrance, that I might love you by My Spirit. Do not fear, for Mine is not a fleshly love, but a heavenly love. It is unlike anything you have ever known. Be still now as I reveal Myself to You. Be still in the presence of your God.

I love you.

His Presence

I am the One you can count on. When all others fail, I will prevail. Oh, how I hunger for you to want Me. How I love you! I choose to inhabit in the very midst of your worship of Me. How I long for the day that we will be together face to face. Oh, how I long for you.

Tell others what I am telling you, that they

might know. For Mine is a love of weightlessness; it is a love of uplifting compassion. This I am freely giving to you. All you need to do is receive.

So I ask you today—will *you* receive Me?

From The Author

Is Jesus Christ the love of your life, deep within your heart? If not, today could be your day to finally know Him! Yes, your heart has been touched by the wonderful, God-given writings in this book, but they are only an appetizer compared to the full meal God your Father has prepared for you in His Book, the Bible—which is Jesus Christ, the Word of God, on paper. His Word holds every answer that you will ever need to get through this life on earth.

Now is the time to allow the Holy Spirit to touch your spirit, so that they might unite and become one, just as Jesus is one with the Father. Wouldn't you like to know your God intimately?

Let the following memo serve as your invitation so you might receive Jesus Christ as *your* Lord and Savior.

Memorandum

To: The reader
Date: Today
Time: Now
Occasion: Salvation

*You are hereby cordially invited
to sit at the banquet table
of the King.*

Directions:

1. Open your heart and mind.

2. Ask Jesus: "Come into my heart and cleanse me from all my sins."

3. Acknowledge Jesus as your Lord and Savior: "Thank You for dying on a cross for me. Now, one day, I will live eternally in heaven with You.

4. Ask God to reveal His purpose for your life, so you can start doing *the very thing* you were born to do.

5. Read your Bible every day. Carefully choose a Christian church.

If you have accepted this invitation, Congratulations! Today is your day of salvation—today is your birthday! (John 3:3; Jeremiah 29:11; Isaiah 55:1-3)

ACKNOWLEDGMENT

My Creator

My Father

My Teacher

My Life

The messages in this book were given to me by the Holy Spirit. He used my pen as an instrument for His words. By allowing and yielding my mind and will completely to Him, these pages were written for myself and others, so that we may know His concerns today. I take no credit at all in this work—He alone deserves the praise.